KIRSTEN AMUNDSEN

is
Assistant Professor of Government
at
Sacramento State College
Sacramento, California

THE SILENCED MAJORITY

Women and American Democracy

KIRSTEN AMUNDSEN

Prentice-Hall, Inc. *Englewood Cliffs, N.J.*

A SPECTRUM BOOK

To Sven and Eric

C-13–810291-0
P-13–810283-X

Library of Congress Catalog Card Number 70-153441

Printed in the United States of America

Current printing (last number):
10 9 8 7 6 5 4 3 2 1

Prentice-Hall International, Inc. (*London*)
Prentice-Hall of Australia, Pty. Ltd. (*Sydney*)
Prentice-Hall of Canada, Ltd. (*Toronto*)
Prentice-Hall of India Private Limited (*New Delhi*)
Prentice-Hall of Japan, Inc. (*Tokyo*)

ACKNOWLEDGMENTS

The stimulus for this book came, of course, from the sisters involved in the fight for women's liberation and the many excellent writings and illuminating discussions I've been exposed to since the movement "took off" a couple of years ago. Though my own involvement with the issue is of long standing, it was the renewed political activities on the part of feminists that spurred me on in this project. The virtually total neglect on the part of my discipline, political science, in regard to the "woman question" in America provided whatever additional motivation was needed.

Specifically, thanks are owed to Tina Said and Joy Andrew Huelster who assisted me in digging out the essential data. Typing of the manuscript was done by Meredith Crown and Susan Cohen. All four offered valuable criticism for parts of the book.

I owe thanks as well to friends and to my sons, who bore with my one-track mind in this period and helped restore my balance and sense of humor with their sympathetic attention and occasional salty remarks!

CONTENTS

vii

One

THE AMERICAN WOMAN

Myth and Reality

There is a familiar image of the American woman. We know it from private jokes and public commentary, from the popular magazines and the daily press, from Hollywood comedies and TV series. And we know it, above all, from advertising, in each of the media and in all possible variations.

The American woman, in this widely accepted folklore, is quite a remarkable creature. Young—or at least youngish, pretty, slender, and stylish, she spends a great deal of her time just making herself or keeping herself attractive for the man—or men—in her life. If she isn't busy changing her hair color or hairdo to catch or keep her man, she may be found tending to the vitally important tasks of keeping her skin soft, her figure slim, or her body from having any but the nicest, most enticing odor. Her main problem in life is pleasing the American man and he, in his benevolence, provides her with all the leisure and affluence to make such narcissism and comfort possible. While he is out there plugging away the usual eight hours at the office—or sometimes in a manly construction activity— his woman can spend her time at luncheons or coffee-klatches, in dress shops or at the hairdresser's, or, of course, lounging in front of the TV set.

As a homemaker or mother, the American woman is no less astounding. Her house, invariably in surburban rambler or two-story colonial style, is both attractive and immaculately kept. Her

1

floors shine, mirrorlike, from the application of the latest finds in instant waxes; her carpets are as plush and soft as they are spotless; her kitchen is as gleaming as it is well-ordered and studded with appliances and gadgets. Her kids, the darling little mischiefs, may be around to mess it all up a bit, it is true. But with efficient use of the new super-aids for housekeeping and cleaning, the responsibilities of motherhood and homemaking are made as easy as they are gratifying.

The American woman, according to the Madison Avenue stereotype, comes across as a very lucky being indeed. Loved, protected, and indulged, she is safe from the vagaries and challenges of the cold, cruel world out there. She does have duties, of course, but they are all of the pleasant, feminine kind. For her, the problem is not to explore, to compete, to survive in an environment of constant turmoil and bewildering change; she is simply to remain a woman or to become even more of one to the satisfaction of the man or men in her life.

There is, we must admit, a companion image of this most fortunate and endearing representative of the species. It is that of the American woman as a scheming, grasping, selfish female, hoarding most of the wealth of this country. This view is held by a good number of the "locker-room" boys, but expressed by many, many more in "men's" jokes, in half-serious conversations, and in dead-serious attempts to discredit the challenges of feminists. Women own this country, it is said. They have attained great wealth and power not through their own work and accomplishments, but by cleverly exploiting the grossly unfair divorce laws or by merely surviving their hard-pressed, overworked mates. In marriage, in the courts, in the social environment in general, the American woman knows how to hold her own and get her way. Manipulating, coy, and bitchy, she can outmaneuver the all-American boy, the poor clod, almost any time she sets her mind to it. She has to be guarded against this formidable creature—she must not be allowed to take all of the reins. The problem with the American woman, in the minds of millions of resentful, put-upon men, is that "She has it too good!"

These two common visions intermingle at times, testifying to a truly disturbing degree of confusion and irrationality concerning woman's role. Eve, the darling wife and mother, embodying all the proper and appealing feminine traits, can suddenly become Eve, the bitch, the coy and cold manipulator, the overbearing ruler of home, hearth, and country. The preferred stereotype, the devoted homemaker, is on occasion seen as drab, harassed, and ailing; but this condition is presumably a temporary one, to be quickly and easily relieved by use of the proper products, benefits of Madison Avenue and the ever-providing husband. Depending on their mood or the issue at hand, American men—and women, too—switch from one view to the other; but in the most widely shared conception of the role of women and the nature of sex relations in the United States the underlying assumption is that the American woman is the one who is better off—she has most of the advantages, rightly or wrongly.

To be sure, *men, too,* can be slighted and maligned in their stereotyped portrayals in the mass media. In television commercials and situation comedies, in particular, the American man is often portrayed as a naive and clumsy dependent of the female of the species. For status, for sex, for services, or for comfort he will turn to women, ever to women, albeit of very different types. His need to win the approval of and/or capture women seemingly drives him to buy ever bigger and better cars and a multitude of questionable items to project a "masculine" image. It must be kept in mind that stereotypes generally serve the purpose of manipulation. In advertising the goal is obviously to promote consumerism and for that purpose the present insecurity and tension of sex relations in America serve eminently well. What could better promote an incessant drive for status and affluence than perpetual and not so subtle suggestions that women are both desirable and materialistic, demanding and fickle? To have them love him and to keep them in the style conveyed by the media as acceptable, a man will have to achieve a great deal indeed. His resentment of this plight is not likely to lessen if the woman for whom all this is being done turns out to be at times less than totally exciting and satisfying. And if she turns out to be among the ungrateful ones and claims a life of her own and a need for some privacy and independent achievement in the midst of this suffocating attention and service to her "feminine" needs, then his resentment can quickly turn to anger—a puzzled anger, perhaps—that anyone who has it *that good* should not just gracefully accept her easy and comfortable role.

Women at work, women trying to make careers for themselves in fields where they have to mix with men, are conspicuously caught in the "damned if you do and damned if you don't" vise created by this attitude. If they are vital and assertive, Alice Rossi points out, they will be rejected as "aggressive bitches out to castrate men." Yet if they are quiet and unassuming, they will be rejected as "unlikely to amount to much." [1] Sweetness-and-light talk and flattery and gratitude to bosses and male colleagues will ease their acceptance into the field, but then they find that they are rejected for promotion because they lack ambition and drive.

Most have learned to play the game. Quiet acceptance, withdrawal from competition, and behind-the-scenes fuming are the common responses among women. And men, as a consequence, may continue to pat themselves on the back for being friends and protectors of the "proper" women, just as they are the rightful and righteous defenders of the male prerogatives against the masculinized, frigid, castrating females who dare to persist in their attacks against those prerogatives.

No wonder, then, that there is shock and anger that an increasing number of women in this country are voicing loud and bitter complaints! It has become obvious to even the most casual observer of the social scene that we are now faced with a rebirth of insurgency among women. NOW (National Organization of Women), Redstockings, Women's Equity League, WITCH (Women's International Conspiracy from Hell), and last, but not least, Women's Liberation have captured the attention of the media and the public—and with a vengeance. Tens of thousands of American women are estimated to be members of one or another of the new feminist groups now proliferating around the country. Although the methods advocated and the styles of action chosen are widely different, the aim

1. Alice S. Rossi, "Job Discrimination and What Women Can Do about It," *Atlantic Monthly* (March, 1970), pp. 99–103.

of all these groups is essentially the same: to break her shackles and free the American woman—socially, economically, and psychologically.

The reaction to these strange new stirrings in the ranks of females has inevitably been negative on the part of the majority within both sexes. Given the stereotyped images of the American woman, one could expect none but the most uncomprehending and bitter responses to her new claims for equality, for justice, and for the freedom of the "other" half of the species. "What does woman want? Dear God, what does she want?" exclaimed none other than Sigmund Freud early in this century. His exasperated cry is now echoed by millions of Americans. Now that she has the vote, too, what does she want indeed?

So powerful are the images created by the media that until very recently only a handful of social observers could point to signs of serious disturbances and dissatisfaction among American women. Until the new wave of feminism hit this country—nearly a half a century after the original Suffragettes won the big prize and retired from the bitter and brutal struggle—commentaries on the social and economic inequities affecting women were few and far between. Perceptive and penetrating analyses like Helen Hacker's "Women as a Minority Group" [2] and Alice Rossi's "Inequality between the Sexes" [3] were largely ignored. It was the angry and devastating exposé of the Madison-Avenue-fostered housewife syndrome, Betty Friedan's *The Feminine Mystique*,[4] that opened the way for a new dialogue on the important and neglected topic of woman's place and woman's rights in American society.

The response of women readers to *The Feminine Mystique* was a telling one. Despite the largely negative reviews by critics, nearly all of them male, the book made the best-seller list shortly after it hit the bookstores in the fall of 1963 and has gone through several printings since. Betty Friedan wrote primarily about and for the middle-

2. Helen Hacker, "Women as a Minority Group," *Social Forces*, no. 3 (1951).

3. Alice S. Rossi, "Inequality between the Sexes," in R. J. Lifton, ed., *The Woman in America* (Boston: Houghton Mifflin Co., 1964), pp. 106–19.

4. Betty Friedan, *The Feminine Mystique* (New York: Dell Publishing Co., 1963).

and upper-middle-class housewife with a college background, and there can be no question that she reached her audience. In these circles, her name was soon a household word. Deeply resented, hotly debated, and fiercely mocked though her thesis was, it nevertheless exerted a fascination that can only be explained by its exposure of issues that touched the raw nerves and guts of both women and men.

The prevalent image of the happy, fulfilled, and secure housewife is bunk—pure bunk, said Betty Friedan. The American woman is instead cajoled, manipulated, and brainwashed into accepting the role of wife and mother as the only possible and proper outlet for her talents and energies. Stifled, bored, and frustrated, she eventually takes refuge in daydreaming, drinking, and neurotic activity of various kinds, unconscious that there may be genuine alternatives to spending one's days by the kitchen sink and stove.

Since Friedan's trail-blazing inquiry into the happy housewife myth, publication of new works and of data gathered by official agencies, particularly the Woman's Bureau of the U.S. Department of Labor, have brought to the fore facts that profoundly challenge the stereotyped images of American women. And as the new feminism began to surface in 1969 and 1970, it became clear that this cherished folklore was destined to be shattered beyond repair. The data were too overwhelming, the offense too obvious, and the injury too grave for the myth to persist, no matter what the attempts of the advertising industry or the media in general.

What the current literature reveals is that the life situation of a near majority of American women bears virtually no resemblance to the images so dear to Madison Avenue. These stereotypes are totally unrealistic, new feminists point out. Worse, they are hypocritical and dishonest and do grave damage both to the feminist cause and to the psyches of individual women. Attention must be paid to the stark and bleak realities confronting tens of millions of American women today. Attention must be paid to the injustice, to the frustrations, to the limitations imposed on women generally—which thereby affect the very quality of life in this society.

There is an urgency in this claim that, given its exclusive focus, leads many to question its validity today. But what is being discussed *is,* after all, a long overdue redress of a major injustice against half of our people and the updating and change of images that contort and betray reality. To make this claim is not to suggest that men in this society are generally subject to fair and decent treatment either on the job market, in political life, or in the media. The existence of poverty among roughly one-fifth of Americans, male and female, and the lack of economic security and poverty of social services for tens of millions of Americans in the labor force all give evidence of a socioeconomic system that permits serious inequities and patterns of exploitation to affect large groups within its population. The point to be made here, however, is that women *by themselves* constitute just such an exploited group, by far the largest and, as will be shown, the most unfairly treated. Yet—and equally striking— there is far less recognition of the true socioeconomic and political situation of women than there is of the position of other "out-groups" in American society.

Poverty in America has been exposed; the problem of racial minorities is being explored; the frustrations and insecurities of male workers, both of the blue-collar and white-collar variety, have also been given reasonably sympathetic and thorough treatment. But women's status, women's opportunities, and women's share of power in this democracy are but rarely the subject of serious discussions. The very suggestion that this presents a problem is all too often met with consternation and ridicule by both laymen and scholars. We will suggest, however, that the nature, dimensions, and consequences of this problem have an impact on our daily lives that is as misperceived as it is formidable. It is of the utmost importance, therefore, that it be explored and that it be *named.* Then, and only then, can we attend to the social problems both sexes have in common within the framework of a group or class analysis.

I.

To a social analyst, the primary task ahead must be to explode the myths shrouding what are the realities of life for the majority of American women. Their supposed affluence and ease of life, their protected status, their power, their sexual inferiority and "penis envy" are but some of the common perceptions that have to come under scrutiny. The most unsparing look must be cast at what *is* known and at what *may be* inherent and unchangeable in the situation and in the nature of women. Where a myth is hollow it must be exposed as such; where a stereotype betrays the truth it must be discarded. Be the commitment an ideological or an intellectual one, the problem at hand requires a systematic and relentless exposition of the facts of the situation.

Immediately, it is the invidious and shallow portrayals of women in the media that call for our attention: woman as sexpot, woman as helpmate, woman as ever the object of man's desires and of his protective and indulgent care. How does this perception hold up under the harsh glare of reality? To what extent, if any, does it conform to the truth? Let us take but a brief look at the data coming our way at this time, which suggest that reality is radically different from the myth.

First of all, it must be recognized that women in America are no longer primarily housewives. In fact, more than 31 million adult women are now at work. They constitute at this time about 40 percent of our total work force.[5] Seventy-five percent of these women earn salaries of less than $5,000 yearly. Half of them, nearly 15 million women, have to make do on less than $3,700 yearly. Less than 2 percent have average incomes of more than $10,000 yearly.

And what is life really like for these tens of millions of women whose very existence challenges the common vision of American womanhood? Could it be that a majority of them work for pleasure, and not out of necessity? Are their strikingly low incomes used

5. Data pertaining to women in the labor force are from the U.S. Bureau of the Census and the U.S. Department of Labor, the Women's Bureau.

mainly to supplement that of the head of the family? Might they be motivated to take a job simply out of a desire for a few extra comforts and luxuries and possibly, also, because they had too much free time on their hands?

No. We find that 7.8 million of the married working women have husbands who earn less than $5,000 yearly, and over half of these have children under the age of 18 at home. Work for them is a compelling necessity. For the single female workers, 6.5 million in all, it is almost without exception the need for money that drives them into the job market. Another 5.8 million women workers are widowed, divorced, or separated, and nearly all of these are the main support not just of themselves, but of their families. Startlingly, 2.4 million of these working women fall in the category of the poor in the United States.[6] And among them, they have 4.5 million children to support.

Women who work out of necessity, women who work for *compelling* economic and *not* frivolous or "selfish" reasons, number, then, more than 20 million in the contemporary United States. A substantial group, one must admit. We need not inquire much further as to the reasons why the other 11 million women are on the job market—it is enough to point out that the majority of them have husbands whose incomes are between $5,000 and $8,000 per year—over the poverty level, but below the level defined as "comfortable" by government economists. But of the more than 20 million who clearly *must* work to lift themselves and their families out of the poverty category, how do their lives conform to the stereotyped images perpetrated by the media?

If they are women with children at home (and about *12 million* of them are), the comforts, the leisure, and the self-indulgence supposedly typical of the American woman will be virtually unknown to them outside the pictures flashed on movie and TV screens or brandished in newspaper and magazine ads. What they experience in their everyday existence is incessant toil and serious

6. "Poverty" here being defined as an income of $3,335 or less for an urban family of four. (Molly Orbansky, "The Poor in City and Suburb," *Social Security Bulletin* [December, 1966], pp. 1–16.)

deprivation, not just of the luxuries, but of some of the very essentials of a decent life in contemporary America. They are likely to live in substandard housing units—cramped, cluttered, and poorly furnished. The television set will be there, without a doubt, and so will the refrigerator and, in all likelihood, a washing machine. But the other amenities of the typical American life will be gone—no plush carpeting, no gleaming and smart tile floors, no heavy luxurious draperies, and no super, all-new appliances and gadgets to make housework a breeze and cooking a pleasure. The dingy little apartment, the run-down old house, or the flimsy, cheap little bungalow contains nothing to give visual pleasure or to offer bodily comfort; it is, instead, bleak to look at and hard to keep up, adding to the strain of the invariable and tiring hours of housework awaiting these 12 million women when they arrive home from their eight-hour-a-day jobs in shops, in the fields, in factories, in laundry services, or in households.

Twelve million American women. Twelve million who, with their families, lead lives that belie the vision of America as a woman's paradise, that belie the very American dream.

And what about the rest? What about the additional 11 million women at work today? About 2 percent are well enough off, as indicated earlier; 2 percent of women working earn yearly salaries of $10,000 or more. Little more than a *half a million* women are in that relatively fortunate class. The other 10.5 million have salaries far below this figure. For these women, however, the income is supplemental to one that has already lifted the family out of the poverty category. The money brought home by the wife *might* then be used for amenities and luxuries of the kind presumed by the media to exist in every American home.

Yet, as any middle-class American will recognize, even an income of $10,000–$11,000 does not connote real affluence today. There are the questions of medical bills, of college education for the children, of insurance, to mention just a few of the items that inexplicably drain the budget of most Americans today. Most of the 10.5 million women we are presently concerned with are struggling to make do with family budgets of well under $9,000 per year.[7] Not an easy job, that. Hardly one that allows for the self-indulgence, the pampering, and the superior comforts supposedly available to the American woman.

For all these working women with families to maintain, all 24.5 million (with the exception of the less than 1 percent lucky enough to have household help), the daily existence is characterized by work, duties, errands, and worries: an endless and exhausting round of activities that, while for many preferable to the stay-at-home life, leaves them with little time and less energy for the pleasantries, the fun, the self-indulgence coming their way in Madison Avenue's vision of the life of the American woman. It is toil, pure and simple, for the great majority. Research conducted in recent years has found that working wives average 68 working hours weekly,[8] all of that for very little pay and, all too often, precious little appreciation.

But we have only begun. We have not even looked at the millions of women who find themselves both without jobs and without husbands in our society today. Deprived of the minimal security and dignity that either work or marriage might offer, they find themselves prey to the prejudices and highhanded manipulation of the welfare establishment. Over three-quarters of welfare recipients in major cities are women. They receive welfare payments largely through the Aid to Dependent Children Programs and, with too few exceptions, in that program the rule is that a woman may not get her allowance if a man can be found to share the sorry premises inhabited by her and her children. If you are a woman and you are poor, as are millions of women today, you are supposed to do without sex as well as without comfort, security, and privacy!

The American woman is, then, both misperceived and maligned in the cliché-ridden views conjured up by the media. Underpaid,

7. Suggested by the Bureau of Labor Statistics as "moderate" for standard city families in 1967.

8. According to a study of housewives in Syracuse, N.Y., quoted in *Sheryn's Nifty Newsletter,* I, no. 1 (May, 1970), p. 1. Also, Chase Manhattan Bank estimates a woman's *overall* work week to be 99.61 hours.

overworked, and often left with the main responsibility and toil of rearing a family, she is anything but the secure and sheltered, pleased and pampered little doll winking at you from underneath triple nylon lashes on the TV screen. Being a woman in this society at this point in time means having to deal with all of the risks, all of the challenges, and all of the responsibilities supposed to be the man's province. Moreover, it means taking upon oneself "woman's work." The only difference is that for the work women do, they will be paid less and they will advance far more slowly, if at all, *and* they will be virtually closed out of a number of professions—the highest-paying ones and the ones carrying the greatest status.

It is this situation, the deteriorating condition of women in America, together with the increasing spread of egalitarian ideas, that has led to the resurgence of feminism in the seventies. What is now demanded is an end to the domination and exploitation of 53 percent of the citizens of this democracy. What is sought is a greater measure of equality, an opening up of opportunities, a widening of options for women. What may be achieved, it is suggested, will be a new life style for both women and men, and upgrading of the quality of life in the society in general, on the social, economic, and political levels.

It will be the thesis of this book that whether one's focus is on the false and demeaning stereotypes, on the inequities of the job market and in educational institutions, or on the numerous norms and habits limiting the choices of women everywhere, one will eventually have to deal with political structures and with representation within these same structures. The relationship between the sexes in America is most likely to be changed through political action, as are the relationships between the races and between different classes or strata within the society. It is through politics, after all, that one gets the rules and regulations, the important legislation that determines wages and working conditions, that guarantees access and opportunities, and that provides for the necessary services enabling women as well as men to fully develop and utilize their talents and skills. It is also, ultimately, politics that will change institutions and the social conditioning structuring both the male and female personality in this society. And it is mainly through politics that one can hope to rebuild values and to change the blatantly counterfeit stereotypes of women that now get in the way of understanding and appreciating their true situation and their genuine needs.

II.

This, it is true, is likely to be a highly controversial proposition. It will surely be contended, now as in the past, that woman's role in society and our conception of it, is rooted in biological distinctions, inherent psychological traits, and social necessities. It will be said that it is simply not in woman's nature to compete on an equal basis with men in the fields of activity now dominated by the "stronger" sex, nor is it in the interests of society that she do so; that the stock figures of woman as wife, homemaker, and mother have their base in the very natural and commendable disposition of women to conform to those roles; that these are roles, moreover, that have to be performed by women for the continuance of the essential functions of the family—the breeding and rearing of the young and their orderly induction into society.

But this argument no longer has the ring of truth in it. We must, in the first place, contend with the fact that women in America do not now enjoy, and have not for quite some time—if indeed ever —enjoyed, in perpetuity that exclusive and protected position presumed to be theirs. At least one half of American women have to and do work outside the home for the larger portion of their lives.

In the second place, the condition of being a woman has changed drastically, as has the life situation of all individuals, with the coming of the technological revolution. There is, for instance, the dramatic and significant improvement in standards of living, leading to standards of longevity enjoyed only by the privileged few in past centuries. The life expectancy of women in America is now 76 years. At the age of 30, most American women have borne their last child; at the age of 35, all of their children will be in school. Consider, then, the implications of this change: when women are relieved of the need to watch and care for their children in the daytime hours, they have some 35 or more adult years to look forward to. What are they to do with themselves?

The development and increased availability of oral contraceptives has introduced yet another factor into the equation. For the first time in history, women can choose for themselves when, how often, and *if* they want to become mothers. This power alone has the potential to start a veritable revolution in the relationship between the sexes. No longer does woman have to face a future of *"Kinder, Küche, und Kirche."* She may choose it, by all means, but she can also choose to have a full life as a sexual being without being confined to the traditional role of mother and homemaker. Or she may choose to relegate these experiences to a period of her life when she is emotionally, intellectually, and financially ready for them.

The novelty of these circumstances cannot be overemphasized. The role of housewife and mother was central to a woman's experience and dominated all of her adult life up to this century for the very simple reason that when she was finally through with the bearing and rearing of children she had precious few years left to live. At the same time, housework in the past required more effort and a great deal more physical energy than it does now. Quite apart from the socialization process, which, of course, precluded the choice of any other profession for a "well-adjusted" woman, how could one expect women in their forties with little more than a decade of life ahead to pick up the pieces of their fragmented existence and recreate themselves as career-seekers, professionals, craftsmen, or artists in a world both strange and hostile to them? It is remarkable, indeed, that some of them did.

Today, however, even the most dedicated housewife is apt to be plagued by doubts, by boredom, by a stifling sense of frustration in contemplating all those years ahead spent doing the same menial tasks and the unimportant busy work. She will also, if she is reasonably socially aware, be bothered by the fear of having to rely on her own resources at some time in the future. More than two-thirds of American housewives end up on the job market later in their life—very often out of necessity and almost always without any decent preparation for their new roles.

To say, then, that woman's place is in the home is simply to be hopelessly out of touch with the realities of life as well as the potential for change in the experiences of women in America. Although it is true that most women still see, or prefer to see, themselves in the role of mother and homemaker, this is proof of nothing else than that there is a gap between the common perceptions of the American woman and her essential characteristics and circumstances. It is a gap as wide as that splitting the generations apart, and it is every bit as portentous. It cannot be bridged, moreover, until we undergo a process of re-education with regard to the real situation—social, economic and political—of women in this society and with regard to their actual needs and newly found possibilities in these same areas.

How does one set about re-educating a people in something as fundamental as its views on sex relations and family life? Independent opinion-wielders can contribute to some small extent, provided they have access to the media that gets the messages through to people. But for these messages to come with the frequency and in the form necessary to change fundamental values, nothing less than a broadly based and clearly focused social movement is required. For if we are to change the common image of woman in this society, and by "we" I mean those of us among both sexes committed to seeking such change, we will have to capture control of the media and of the educational institutions that are now responsible for the creation of these images. Beyond that, we will have to have sufficient control over decision-making on the governmental level to make the changes necessary for women to enjoy equal status and equal opportunities on the job market and in higher education. We will have to push through the social legislation necessary to free women for greater and more creative efforts in their chosen activities—primarily, establishment of child-care centers, provision for maternal leaves, and abolition of abortion laws.

Can it be done? There are doubters and there are cynics and there are gleeful satirists all ready to cast aspersions on the goals and the potential of the new feminists. But in a society that remains open, where challengers and rebels have a chance to seek and attract support for their cause, much can be achieved through the proper study and application of politics. It is one of the great anomalies of the situation of women today that so very, very few students of politics have attempted a serious analysis of their political situation and how it can be changed. That, it would seem, is a prerequisite to the transformation of values and of life styles that is so hotly desired, yet so dimly perceived, by the new feminists.

What follows is an effort to satisfy that prerequisite.

III.

The basic assumption underlying this analysis will be that it is both morally indefensible and socially damaging to have a major group of citizens in a political democracy denied access to, and opportunities for, socioeconomic benefits and political power. It is morally indefensible because of our expressed commitment to the moral equality of every man and woman in our society and because of the belief widely shared among us, incessantly called upon to rationalize existing inequalities, that our institutions are so arranged as to maximize opportunities for all. And it is socially damaging, first, because of the waste of skill and talent that is involved when a substantial group of citizens is systematically prevented from the development and use of its potential and, second, because pervasive discrimination on the basis of differences created by birth frequently fosters resentment and antisocial behavior in the socially inferior group to the point where the health and stability of the society is endangered.

Insofar as this study is based on the above assumption, it is not "objective." It is very doubtful whether any social analysis—particularly of contemporary problems—can be. Questions posed, arrangement and interpretation of data, determination of what to exclude as well as what to include are all decided on the basis of a certain predisposition to look for some facts rather than others. The view of our eminent international colleague, Gunnar Myrdal, is surely valid, that integrity and scholarship in the social sciences is best served by the explicit recognition of the analysts' own values in conjunction with a searching and profound examination of the dominant values of the society under study.[9] The task of the scholar is quite naturally lightened if he should happen to share in the latter. And so it is in the case at hand. "The American Creed," in Myrdal's phrase, that whole body of core beliefs and values shared by all Americans, is also ours[10] (see Appendix 1).

Another assumption requires clarification at this point; it is superfluous perhaps for fellow students in the social sciences, but important for many individuals outside this field. It has become a commonplace to say that we are all products of the society in which we live. What this means, in the minimal sense, is that attitudes, habits, and predispositions are socially determined. Talents and intelligence, as well as emotional proclivities, make a difference for the individual and it *is* possible for one person to transcend some of the limitations imposed on her by both the socialization process and the social setting. *But* the differential behavior of whole groups in terms of achievements and style of life is to be explained not in terms of inherited mental, emotional, or physical characteristics, but rather in terms of their distinct social experiences from early childhood on. Consider, for instance, this example: a black boy growing up in the South in earlier years was likely to act deferential, devious, unassertive, and coy, because his training and life experience made him thus. We have seen the startling change in black youngsters in this decade and we know full well that there was nothing "natural" about the behavior typically exhibited by

9. See Gunnar Myrdal, *An American Dilemma* (New York: Harper's Brothers, 1944).
10. Ibid.

southern blacks in the past. No one can say that blacks in this society have not by now demonstrated their will to independence, their ability to assert themselves, their seriousness, and their determination to end the pervasive discrimination their race has been subjected to throughout history. "Coy," "deferential," and "unassertive" would be most unlikely adjectives to use in describing the young black man of America today!

So it is—or so it may become—with women. The psychological characteristics held to be "typical" of women are likely to be quite simply socially determined. No one knows what "true femininity" is or if it can, indeed, exist except in the realm of the imagination. It is, by and large, the socialization process that is responsible for the mental sets, the emotional dispositions, and the prevalent behavior of women—just as it is for other groups. Behavior need not be biologically determined for women any more than it is for any one race. Although it is undeniably true that pregnancies and childbirth produce both psychological and physiological changes in women, these are not the kind of transformations that affect their mental and creative capabilities over the long run. The question of the "psychology of women" must therefore be taken up anew; the whole notion must be questioned and subjected to the most searching scrutiny. Only psychologists, anthropologists, and sociologists can fully examine this most abused topic, and only a few have started the re-examination so long overdue. Their findings will be discussed in the latter part of this work. Meanwhile, let me emphasize that this investigation of the "woman question" is undertaken on the assumption that women differ from men in physical characteristics and in mental and emotional dispositions, but that only the former constitute inherent differences. As to potential, ability, or achievement in any one field, it has not yet been proven that women cannot be the equals of men. Nor that they will not—in a different social setting—aspire to become just that.

Two

ON HER OWN
Down and Under

If the American woman is no longer a mere appendage to her man, socially and economically speaking; if she cannot from now on rely on consistent or sufficient support and security in her role of housewife and mother, then what *is* her actual position in American society today? If the stereotyped images of the American woman are false, then what image would conform to the true picture of the situations she now finds herself in? Is it that of woman as a full participant, a social equal, and an accepted competitor to man in the realms of education, work, and politics? Can her conspicuously sorry state as a wage-earner and her relative lack of achievements in most areas of endeavor be ascribed to the fact that she has only recently chosen to take upon herself the challenges, risks, and burdens of work that were formerly relegated to men only? May her grave socioeconomic problems be due to her being a newcomer to the job market? And do we then simply have to wait for her to catch up with the American man in training, skills, and experience for these same problems to be solved?

It should be useful and it could be essential for a genuine understanding of the situation of working women in America—all 31.1 million of them (as of January, 1970)—that their positions in the stratification system of our society be correctly assessed. It may be essential, for that matter, for the comprehension of the whole "woman question." Whatever one may think about the causes and determinants of the relationship between the sexes, it is clear that the roles undertaken by women in contemporary society and the status ascribed to those roles cannot help but affect the interaction, the orientations, the emotional play between men and women. It will, at the very least, influence the form and quality of their relationship. For those who feel an urgent need for change, as well as for those who simply want to cling to the status quo, it is of crucial importance that it be known if, how, and why the 44 percent of women on the job market[1] are assigned to ranks different and distinct from those of men holding formally equivalent positions. We need not for the moment look at the complex question of ranking between men and women in the family; since most married women will be employed outside the home before retirement age, the findings concerning *women at work* might have an impact on one's evaluation of the whole social system.

It should be abundantly clear that a systematic hierarchy of social positions does exist in American society and that we treat the occupants of these positions as superior, equal, or inferior in socially important respects (see Appendix 2). But in considering a modern system of social stratification, one must pay attention to several different dimensions. It is widely believed that we no longer have the obvious and close correlation between economic inequality and differences in authority, power, and prestige that characterizes older class systems. If we are to fix the position of major groups of women in our stratification system, we must look at their rankings in terms of three crucial dimensions—class, status, and power. We must also examine what social mobility is available for women, that is, what are their actual possibilities of moving up and down the class, status, and power hierarchies.

It is quite a novel idea—so far merely hinted at in the social sciences—that women constitute social strata distinct from men occupying formally identical or similar positions in the social hierarchy. Notably, in spite of the many indications at hand that women are treated differently in all the important dimensions, neither sociology nor political science has so far found it opportune

1. According to the *Wall Street Journal* (June 29, 1969), 44 percent of all women aged 16 and older are either employed or seeking work.

to deal with the problem of women in American society as a problem of social stratification. Women are assumed to share the fates of their men, purely and simply. Sex positions, in the classic statement, are *nonstratified*. It is this understanding, widely shared among both sexes, that prevents a woman from viewing her lot in life as being due to her membership in a social group, a collectivity defined not just by birth but by socially determined distinctions. Women, rightly or wrongly, appear to have no consciousness of the causal connections between their life chances and the stratification system special to their society. If Americans in general are lacking in class consciousness, as is frequently decried or applauded by observers, then American women are startlingly so!

What would be the consequences for women—and for American society in its totality—were such a consciousness to evolve? At the very least, one may safely assume a greater likelihood of concerted political action to right whatever wrongs are committed against women. An increased awareness of the rights of women must, of course, be a precondition for their liberation. Any informed knowledge of systematic discrimination and exploitation of women provides the additional crucial condition of a context in which a coherent system of demands and a strategy to implement them can be developed.

As to the *rights* of women to participate fully in all areas of life in America, there is a great deal of ambiguity in the views found within both sexes. On one idea, however, we find general agreement. Every American should have a chance to achieve the best of which he—or she—is capable. This basic belief has been a lever for social change on many an important occasion in the past. From the Abolitionist movement of the nineteenth century to the labor movement of the twentieth, Americans have vigorously fought for and won rights denied them—*unjustly* denied them—on the basis of the almost universally expressed belief in justice and equality of opportunity in this society. Today there is still a disturbingly wide gap between commitment in theory and practice. But there can be little doubt that the *ideal* continues to inspire and to periodically propel disadvantaged groups into action to shorten this social lag. We have seen the most dramatic and recent example of its power in the struggle of blacks to achieve what has long been their due according to the American creed.

Whether or not the majority of women believe themselves able and entitled to share with men all of the burdens, risks, and opportunities of wage-earners at this point in time is no longer of material importance. *Morally,* at least, they consider themselves as individuals to be of equal worth. Politically, they have also sought and won the right to full participation and representation, and one may assume, when such a basic value has found institutional expression throughout half a century, it has by now been internalized by a good many members of the society affected by it. Briefly, what is significant here is that the ground *has* been prepared, ideologically speaking, for a profound and powerful revolt against serious and systematic injustices against women in the economic, social, and political realms.

Consider what might happen then if the American woman were suddenly enlightened to see that her opportunities, her benefits, and her share in the social goods of the society are likely to be a good deal less than that of the American man? That *just because* she is a woman, her life chances are not only different, but significantly reduced in terms of the whole bundle of benefits and privileges that are socially produced? What might she do, were she to come upon the discovery that she is persistently arrogated inferior status, given less salary, and afforded fewer chances to call the shots than men no more skilled or able than she? All that at a time when she is more likely to have to go to work to support herself or to help support her family in her mature years—and all that in a country where her full moral worth, her political rights, and the ideal of equality of opportunity have long been *formally* recognized?

1.

But first, can such gross and arbitrary injustice really be documented? All social analysts will agree that where awareness of serious inequities exists among those subject to it, solidarity and group action may follow. One must, however, have a clear view of the *systematic* nature of the injustice. Only when it can be proven to be part and parcel of the whole economic order and not merely haphazard and erratic can it lead to a determined and concerted political thrust on the part of the victims. American women, like their male fellow citizens in the thirties, may have to free themselves of the notion that their misfortunes and maltreatment on the job market are due to nothing more serious than bad luck, typical male prejudice, or individual stupidity and arrogance among their employers. If recognition of common interests among women is to develop and further lead to organization and action on behalf of women, it will have to follow upon a serious and well-publicized analysis of our system of social stratification and of women's positions within it.

What will have to be shown, then, is whether an employed woman —a worker in a factory—with a given amount of training and experience stands to get a significantly lower wage, less opportunity for advancement, and less of a guarantee of keeping her job than a man in the same position. If that can be shown, then clearly women factory workers are relegated to a lower *economic* strata than are men factory workers, and for no other reason than that they are born of the female sex. If, at the same time, we find that a woman factory worker enjoys less esteem on the job or in the community, is subject to more constraints, and is expected to carry heavier social burdens, then obviously women constitute a different and lower *social* strata than men in terms of their relative status. And if a woman factory worker has less of a chance than a man factory worker to influence and determine the behavior of others and fewer opportunities to exercise control over decisions that affect her life and those of others, then she is also in a distinctly lower strata than the man in terms of relative *power*.

These are the three crucial dimensions of social stratification in a modern society. Economics, status, and power constitute the basis for different rankings, presumably not identical, but undeniably closely related. That we should have such systematic hierarchies in our society is something of an embarrassment to democratic ide-

ology. We are saved in our democratic faith, however, by the ex-
pectation that a person is not relegated to one rank or the other
solely because he is born into it. *Social mobility* is a crucial criterion
in the stratification system of a democracy. There simply has to
be a possibility for individuals to move up and down the class,
status, and power hierarchies. If members of a collectivity defined
by birth are persistently and conclusively relegated to lower strata
than are other members of the society, then one is faced with a
flaw, a very serious flaw, in the fabric of democracy. This cannot be.
When we talk about *class* in a democratic society, we view it as a
temporary aggregate of individuals who happen to occupy similar
social positions at a certain time. In the classic definition, class refers to people destined by birth to similar positions and similar life
chances (see Appendix 2). But in contrast to the castelike hierarchies of older states, our system, although admittedly stratified,
is characterized by a high degree of social mobility. Or so it is said.

Blacks in our society have been studied, scrutinized, and subjected to concern and sympathy for more than a decade, because
our attention is now focused on their continuing, and therefore
inexcusable, low rankings in the stratification system. They are at
long last beginning to get the kind of opportunities and assistance
that will make social mobility more than a fictional term within
their group. Browns are now following in their footsteps, and
American Indians are said to be not far behind. But women—
constituting not a minority, but a bare majority of this nation—
have so far received little or no attention from serious scholars in
the field. Indeed, one might say that if the poor constitute an "in-
visible" America, to use Michael Harrington's compelling term,[2]
then women—working women in America—make up the largest
and least known portion of that sad land. There is an abundance
of data pointing out that the problem of women is identical to the
problem of a minority. And there are grave indicators that their
situation may best be described in the terms used to designate the
least fortunate of groups in the rigid class systems of earlier times.

2. Michael Harrington, *The Other America* (New York: The Macmillan Co.,
1963).

The notion of women constituting an "under" class in American society is a startling one, to be sure. Yet it must be entertained, while still held in abeyance, as we take up the analysis of the data that by now point at least partially in that direction.

Again, our first task is to survey the current job market and see if such pervasive and trenchant differences can be discovered in the opportunities and treatment offered men and women that they can only be explained on the basis of a systematic stratification scheme. It is essential that the data be collected and presented in an acceptable analytic framework. It is imperative that we do more than that, however. We have to somehow envision what the figures mean in terms of the pattern and quality of daily life for the tens of millions of women we are concerned with. We must get a glimpse into their routines, their customary problems, their familiar burdens and pleasures. We must begin to describe the faces behind these statistics, to fashion new images of the American woman that are in touch with the realities of today. It may take a novelist or at the very least an anthropologist with the sensitivity and compassion of Oscar Lewis to complete that task.[3] But we must at the very least start.

II.

One additional theoretical problem has to be attended to before we proceed. It will be argued that the lower salaries and reduced opportunities afforded women on the job market do not affect their class standing and status in the society, since women as housewives and daughters enjoy whatever material advantage and prestige is brought to the family by the male breadwinner. Members of the family supposedly share the same rank and are treated as social equals.

The first flaw in this argument has already been exposed. A con-

3. See, for example, Oscar Lewis, *The Children of Sanchez* (New York: Random House, Inc., 1961).

siderable portion of working women are the main supporters not just of themselves, but of their families. In March, 1970, for example, 5.6 million families in the United States were headed by women. That is, 5.6 million women—widowed, divorced, separated, or single—were responsible for raising children in a fatherless family or for supporting parents or other family members.[4] Marriages, it would seem, are less and less "made in heaven" and for life. One out of every three or four marriages today is dissolved; the rate of divorce has been on the increase in the last decades and is still going up. Since women tend to outlive men as well, a good number of them will have to face life as widows even before old age. All of this means that a woman realistically has to figure on entering and staying on the job market in her mature years, no matter how safely ensconced and busily occupied she may presently be as a housewife. The record shows, in fact, that the median age of women in the labor force in 1969 was 39.5.[5] Also, of the 72 million women aged 16 and over in the population, more than half (37 million) had worked at one time or another during the previous year.[6]

Does a divorcee, an abandoned woman, or even a widow continue to enjoy the economic standing and prestige of her former or late mate? Observations suggest not—not at all. With the possible exception of the rare individuals lucky enough to have been born to or to have married great wealth and high status, women left alone in the world have to make it on their own, not just economically, but socially as well. As countless books and articles on the problems of divorcees reveal, very seldom is there a retinue of friends standing by, only rarely does a newly single woman get invitations to social gatherings, and hardly ever are there acceptable and socially promising organizations for her to join. A woman on the loose in her mature years is a social handicap, a potential threat,

4. U.S. Department of Labor, Bureau of Labor Statistics, *Monthly Labor Review* (December, 1970).

5. Robert L. Stein, "Women At Work," *Monthly Labor Review* (June, 1970), p. 17.

6. Ibid., p. 14.

and a dreaded embarrassment to the couples she used to see socially with her former mate. For most women there is no escape from the lonely world of the formerly married other than joining in the frantic activities of a singles club—if any can be found. For *her* there are no fraternal lodges, no sports clubs, no respectable bars, and no hostesses who will welcome her as a valuable addition to the social group. Unless she has unusually high social standing and income, the widow or divorcee will be left to her own resources. She will even find it harder to get credit in stores or to find acceptance as a buyer of a home or a car.

The economic plight of the woman family head is no less severe. Median incomes among all families headed by women (in 1969) was no more than $4,000—that is, about one-third the median income of husband-wife families in the same year.[7] *And,* in most families in which the woman head worked, the level of family income was determined by her earnings. The myth of American women living high on widow's pensions, alimony payments, or child support is effectively exploded by the following figures: the median contribution to family income of women who were family heads was 72 percent in 1968. What this means is that less than 30 percent of the meager income enjoyed by these 5.6 million single women with children or other family members to support came from the late husband, the ex-husband, the father, or any other source.[8]

Even more sobering is the discovery that of the women struggling to support a family without the help of a husband, 2.4 million live in poverty with the 4.5 million children who are their sole responsibility. (We use here a definition of poverty which is conservative in the eyes of many critics—an income of $3,535 for an urban family of four, as of 1968.) Three out of every five children in families headed by women are poor. In fact, if we accept the economists' figure of $4,855 as designation of the "near-poor" urban family in 1969, we find that this is *above* the median income among all families headed by women.

7. Ibid. Median income for two-parent families in the same year was $11,600.
8. Ibid., p. 17.

The implications of these findings should be clear. An American woman today has to face up to the very real possibility that she may live part or most of her adult life alone. Her chances in that regard are one out of three or four. If she is a widow, the chances of her having to take up work is roughly one out of three, and if she is divorced, two out of three. She is almost more than likely to have children to support in her single state; 77 percent of the working divorcees and 40 percent of the working widows had children under 17 in 1969.[9] At the same time, she will have to face the nasty fact that without a husband on the scene, she and her children are more than likely to live in poverty—even though she works full time in addition to the many, many hours spent on housekeeping and family care.

The supposedly easy living made possible for women through divorce settlement turns out, upon examination, to be a colossal myth. In the most extensive study of divorce yet available, William J. Goode finds that property is split between husband and wife in more than half of the cases, alimony payments are small and relatively infrequent, and the ratio of nonpayment is very high. As to child support, which is of greater significance because of the very limited amount of property to be divided in most cases and also because it represents continuing income, Goode finds the median support payment per family to be a mere $12 per week. In 64 percent of the divorces in Cook County, Illinois, during 1940–1950, the wife was given less than $10 weekly per child. Even more serious was the ratio of nonpayments. Forty percent of the husbands made the payments ordered by the court rarely or not at all; an additional 11 percent made them only "once in a while." And courts, Goode points out, are usually reluctant to jail a husband for nonpayment.[10]

These are not happy prospects. They are, it should be clear, alarming enough for every American woman to take notice and to seek change in the fate that might quite easily be hers in the

9. Mollie Orbansky, *Who Was Poor in 1966*, Research and Statistics Note No. 23 (Department of Health, Education and Welfare, December, 1967).
10. William J. Goode, *After Divorce* (Glencoe, Ill.: The Free Press, 1956), pp. 220–23.

years ahead. Although there has been some decrease in the incidence of poverty, the latest figures show that for white mothers who were the main support of their families and who worked full time the year around, the median earnings were still no more than $4,855 (as of March, 1969).[11] That puts them squarely in the category of the "near poor" in an urban area. Black mothers struggling with a year-round job and saddled with the main support of their families were even worse off: their median earnings were only $3,235 in 1969—$200 under the poverty figure for that year.[12]

In all, among families headed by white women, one-quarter are now in poverty. Among families headed by black women, more than half are in poverty. The comparative figures for men show that less than a quarter of families headed by black men are in poverty and less than 7 percent of those headed by white men are in poverty.[13]

What is particularly startling about these figures is that they pertain to two classes of people that supposedly command great sympathy among Americans—women trying to raise families on their own and children growing up in fatherless homes. Together they made up more than one-quarter of all poor in the United States in 1966—about 7 million of the 25.9 million people living in poverty.

We are still not through exploring the economic risks facing American women who live without husbands. As of March, 1969, there were 12,303,000 of these women in the labor force.[14] There were, in addition, several million lone women subsisting on welfare, on Social Security, or on old-age pensions. It is widely known that most welfare recipients are women who receive their aid through the Aid to Dependent Children Program. In fact, no less than eight out of every ten welfare recipients in our major cities are women. When we include these women, that is, women on welfare and women over 65, into our consideration here, we find that poor persons residing in families with female heads and female unre-

11. Stein, "Women At Work," p. 17.
12. Ibid., p. 17.
13. "A Matter of Simple Justice," The Report of the President's Task Force on Women's Rights and Responsibilities, April, 1970.
14. Stein, "Women At Work," p. 13.

lated individuals account for all of 41 percent of the total poor in 1968. And that indicates *an increase in the rate of poverty for women* and for persons dependent on women by 15 percent in the last ten years! In 1959, the categories we are talking about made up 26 percent of the total poor.[15]

Aged women living alone constitute another group of individuals supposedly deserving sympathy and help in our society. In reality, however, they frequently suffer a very bitter fate. The lonely aged poor, of which a clear majority are women, are the most impoverished single group in their subculture of poverty, as Michael Harrington points out.[16] Most often they are aged widows with incomes of less than $1,000 yearly. In 1966, the average monthly benefits coming to widows 62 years and over were $60.61. Nearly 2.6 million lone and aged women had to eke out an existence on this allowance. An additional half million lone women over age 72 got even less—$34.94 per month. Although somewhere between two-thirds and three-fourths of the aged in America are now covered by Social Security, the "unrelated individuals" among the poor had only a 37 percent coverage in 1957.[17] Inequities in regard to women still exist in the Social Security system: working wives' contributions are not given fair recognition, for example, according to the President's Task Force on Women's Rights and Responsibilities.[18]

These rough data should be more than sufficient to show that woman's fate in our society today is no longer tied to that of her man to the point where the two may be treated as one inseparable entity in terms of economics and status. Self-supporting women in the labor force and women who are heads of their families add up to such an impressive number that they must be viewed as separate and major groups within the population. At the same time, indications are overwhelming that as groups they are to be found at the bottom

15. U.S. Department of Commerce, Bureau of the Census, "Poverty in the United States, 1959 to 1968," *Current Population Reports*, Series P-60, no. 68 (December 31, 1969), p. 2.

16. Harrington, *The Other America*, pp. 106–7.

17. *1969 Handbook on Women Workers*, Women's Bureau Bulletin 294 (Washington, D.C.: U.S. Department of Labor).

18. President's Task Force, "A Matter of Simple Justice," pp. 11–12.

ranks of the stratification system. The situation is all the more serious because of the fact that this is a fate that *may* in this day and age befall almost any woman at some point in her life. Abandonment, divorce, and widowhood are not rare and infrequent, but rather quite common experiences for the supposedly fairer and weaker of the sexes. And on her own, without the protection of a mate, the American woman has to face risks and accept situations that are evidently harder, much harder, to bear than we have previously thought.

It is very questionable, too, whether it is either morally proper or politically defensible to ignore the seemingly great inequities in jobs and education affecting married women on the grounds that they do, after all, belong in the social strata of their husbands. Not only the instability of marriage today, but also the very real need for the wife's income in many families argues against treating the woman as a mere appendage, socially and economically speaking. In 1968, 38.3 percent of married women were in the labor force, and in 61.3 percent of these families, the husband's yearly income was below $7,000. In more than a quarter of the two-income families, the wife contributed 40 percent or more of the total income.[19] Wives work, more often than not, because they have to—to maintain what is hardly more than a barely decent standard of living in contemporary America.

The plain fact is, in the end, that the sociological conditions and climate of the seventies is different from that of earlier decades. It is time social science catches up—it is high time, indeed, that it catches up with the new and threatening situation confronting the American woman.

III.

What do we find, then, when we focus on the American woman's share of earnings and opportunities on the job market? Is she, as

19. Ibid.

our data so far seem to suggest, incontestably, unconditionally, and irrevocably on the bottom? And is it the stratification system that determines her chance to enjoy what the American man has come to expect once he enters the labor market?

It is clear that the general disparity in income between the sexes is nothing less than dramatic. Sex bias, concludes the prestigious President's Task Force on Women's Rights and Responsibilities, takes a greater economic toll than racial bias. Reporting in April, 1970, the Task Force pointed to the following startling figures:

Table 2.1

MEDIAN EARNINGS FOR FULL-TIME
WORKERS EMPLOYED YEAR ROUND

White men	$7,396
Negro men	4,777
White women	4,279
Negro women	3,194

Source: "A Matter of Simple Justice," The Report of the President's Task Force on Women's Rights and Responsibilities, April, 1970, p. 18.

Another—and equally shock-producing—way of looking at these figures is to view the income of women as a percentage of the income of men. We find then that women earn roughly 58 percent as much as men. The situation has, in fact, deteriorated in the last decades. In 1955 the average American woman engaged in full-time employment earned $63.90 for each $100 earned by the average American man. By 1960, she was earning $60.80 for each $100 he got, and by 1968 her average was only $58.20 per $100.[20]

The main reason for this conspicuous gap is often said to be the difference in the kinds of jobs men and women are likely to hold. More than 64 percent of the women working today are employed as service, sales, or clerical personnel or as domestic servants—and all

20. "Rebelling Women—The Reason," U.S. News and World Report, April 13, 1970, p. 35.

of these are relatively low-paying jobs. Men, on the other hand, find employment as professional and technical workers, managers, proprietors, craftsmen, foremen, factory workers—all jobs that pay better. And 70 percent of men working are employed in these categories.[21]

Although this fact explains the earning gap between men and women to some degree, it does not, by any means, excuse it. What has to be explored is *why* women end up in the lower-paying jobs. In order for us to accept their fate as just and proper in a democratic society, we would have to be shown that women either do not have the capabilities for any other work and/or have no desire for it.

That the first proposition is patent nonsense is in the first place shown by the fact that some women, a significant number in terms of demonstrable ability, have made it into almost every job category dominated by and presumed to be better suited to men. In the United States, these "loophole" women, as Caroline Bird calls them,[22] may be so few in some trades and professions that they could be said to be only exceptions to the rule. But in other modern societies women have moved in *large* numbers into the same fields. In Israel, in the Scandinavian countries, and in the Soviet Union, for example, women have proven themselves as doctors, dentists, engineers, architects, scientists, and skilled technicians and operators for many years. Their most spectacular advances have come in the Soviet Union, where they now constitute 75 percent of the doctors, 83 percent of the dentists, 28 percent of the engineers, and 38 percent of the scientists. The respective percentages for the United States are 6.5, 2.1, 1.2, and 7.[23]

Surely no one is going to argue that the American woman is less talented and capable than the Soviet woman! Given the number of suits filed by women denied access to certain jobs in the last few years, it is going to be equally difficult to defend the theory that American women are not interested in the higher-paid professions.

21. Ibid.
22. Caroline Bird, *Born Female* (New York: Pocket Books, 1969).
23. Cynthia Fuchs Epstein, *Woman's Place* (Berkeley: University of California Press, 1970), p. 12.

To suggest that they are not is, after all, an insult to their good practical sense.

It is worth noting, too, that in one of the most important professions from which women have been virtually excluded, the evidence indicates that they could contribute a great deal indeed. According to the U.S. Department of Labor, two-thirds as many women as men (8 and 12 percent of the population, respectively) have engineering aptitude.[24]

The grave error and disastrous effect of the concept of "masculine" and "feminine" occupations is seen most clearly in the skilled trades and crafts, as Janice Neipert Hedges points out. These are jobs that bring with them high earnings, but where training costs are low. Women make up only 3 percent of the craftsmen and less than 1 percent of the skilled tradesmen of this country. These are simply not "women's jobs"—the prejudice against women here is as deep as it is rampant. And yet, "The basic requirements that run through the skilled trades are finger and hand dexterity and eye-hand coordination [abilities required for typing and many other clerical occupations performed by women], together with aptitude for form and space perception." The particular combination of aptitudes required for a number of crafts are found as frequently among female as male students in the eleventh grade. Nor can strength requirements be considered a real obstacle to women's access to these relatively profitable fields, since most require only light strength. Also, Miss Hedges reminds us, some women are stronger than some men.[25]

We have to conclude, then, that women are in the lower-paid occupations for the simple reason that these are jobs considered "fitting" for women—this is the only rank to which they are welcomed. Moreover, the prejudice in operation here, shared by men and women alike, is not a "natural" one. The fact that it has been wholly or significantly overcome in other societies is sufficient proof of that. It is, one must suspect, due to a bias built into the institutional structure of our society, particularly that part of the structure

24. Stein, "Women At Work," p. 26.
25. Ibid.

endowed with legitimate authority to distribute goods and resources among us.

This is a point we shall return to and dwell on at considerable length. What is suggested here is another way of hypothesizing that the stratification system operates to the definite and disastrous disadvantage of women who have to make it on their own.

One specific example offers an important illustration of this general proposition. Education could and should make for significant differences in the status and earnings of different groups in an "achieving society." Can women's lack of advances on the job market perhaps be attributed to their inadequacies in this regard? Are they simply not prepared—as far as formal education is concerned—to take up competition with men?

Startlingly, the record shows just the opposite. The Department of Labor tells us that women 18 years of age and over in the labor force have slightly more schooling than does the general population.[26] The median years of school completed by women workers is higher than that of men workers.[27]

The full extent of the handicap suffered by educated women is revealed by the following fact: A woman college graduate can expect to earn $446 less per year than a white male who has only graduated from elementary school!

IV.

Sex bias operates throughout the job market. However, the real measure of its effect can still be best obtained through a comparison of income and opportunities afforded each of the sexes in the job categories occupied by both. "Equal pay for equal work" is, after all, a time-honored and all-American principle. To suggest that it is not in operation in regard to the majority of this nation is to fire

26. *Women in the Labor Force,* p. 175.
27. Ibid., p. 178.

Table 2.2

MEDIAN INCOME IN 1966 OF PERSONS 25 YEARS OF AGE AND OVER
(BY EDUCATIONAL ATTAINMENT, SEX, AND COLOR)

Educational Attainment	Women			Men		
	Total	White	Non-white	Total	White	Non-white
Total	$1,926	$1,988	$1,561	$6,128	$6,390	$3,665
Elementary school	1,190	1,236	993	3,488	3,731	2,632
Less than 8 yrs.	1,009	1,005	932	2,784	2,945	2,376
8 yrs.	1,404	1,416	1,303	4,518	4,611	3,681
High school	2,368	2,421	2,057	6,576	6,736	4,725
1 to 3 yrs.	1,913	1,960	1,698	5,982	6,189	4,278
4 yrs.	2,673	2,700	2,475	6,924	7,068	5,188
College	3,569	3,519	3,964	8,779	9,023	5,928
1 to 3 yrs.	2,827	(1)	(1)	7,709	(1)	(1)
4 yrs.	4,165	(1)	(1)	9,728	(1)	(1)
5 yrs. or more	6,114	(1)	(1)	10,041	(1)	(1)

*Source: U.S. Department of Commerce, Bureau of the Census, Current Population Reports,
Series P-60, no. 53.*

(1) Not available.

a very serious charge, indeed, at the socioeconomic structure of this
country. Can it really be true?

Half of all women workers are employed in 21 of the 25 distinct
occupations listed in the Bureau of the Census tabulations. We are,
of course, interested mainly in those shared to some significant extent
by both sexes. In the Current Population reports, thirteen of these
occupations are examined as to salary differences for men and
women in each.[28] The results are as follows: In the category "Professional, technical and kindred workers," *men's* median income
in 1967 was *$9,370* and *women's, $5,210.* To break this down further,

28. Epstein, *Woman's Place*, p. 10.

we can use several examples that are of special importance because of the numbers involved. Male sales workers in the same year earned a median salary of $6,814; female salesworkers, $2,116. Male bank tellers earned from $5.00 to $31 more per week than women doing identical work. We are, of course, talking about full-time work the year round for both sexes.

Service work is another area dominated by women, but with a significant number of men participating as well. When private households are excluded, we find that men grossed a median wage of $4,532 and women a mere $2,076. For laborers, "except mine and farm," the differential was also substantial. Men here earned $3,979 yearly and women only $3,628.

A specific example of the way sex discrimination operates in factories is offered by the textile industry. Almost three-fifths of the women workers here were employed in four occupations that require less skill than the jobs typically held by men. That is not because they could not or would not learn the skills—the number of women who gained access to the higher-paying jobs testified to that. What happens is rather that they are automatically channelled into the lower-paying jobs. Moreover, even for the luckier women, the pay was lower than it was for men. Among Jacquard weavers, for example, the highest paid of the group—men—got $2.19 per hour, whereas the women received only $2.09.

There are numerous other job categories where a woman is given a lower salary than a man regardless of her seniority and qualifications, as Table 2.3 indicates. It is, however, *the low degree of social mobility* afforded women that more than anything else keeps them at the bottom rank of their chosen occupations. In fact, the sex-gap seems to widen in the upper brackets.

Two professions dominated by women offer the most striking illustration of this principle. The domination is in terms of numbers only—in status, salaries, and power, the relatively few men in these occupations outrank their female colleagues persistently and dramatically. They do so because it is *they* who are offered the opportunities, *they* who are awarded the honors, and *they* who are given the responsibilities that carry with them influence and au-

Table 2.3

MEDIAN ANNUAL EARNINGS
OF FULL-TIME WORKERS

Occupation	Women	Men
Scientists	$10,000	$13,200
Professional, technical	6,691	10,151
Proprietors, managers	5,635	10,340
Clerical workers	4,789	7,351
Sales workers	3,461	8,549
Craftsmen	4,625	7,978
Factory workers	3,991	6,738
Service workers	3,332	6,058

Source: U.S. Department of Labor, National
Science Foundation. Data for 1968.

thority. *Formally*, however, salary differentials based on sex in these professions have been abolished.

In the case of *teaching*, for example, where 1.4 million women found employment in 1969, 85 percent of the women were found in elementary school, in the lower grades. Status and pay is slightly lower there than it is in high school, where women compose only 46 percent of the teaching staff. The drop in the percentage of women teaching in secondary schools has been sharp; they constituted 57 percent of high school teachers in 1957. But the decline of women elementary school principals has been really dramatic. John Hoyle offers a very revealing glimpse into the nature of the problem in an article titled "Who Shall Be Principal—A Man or a Woman?" In 1928, 55 percent of elementary school principals were women; in 1948, 41 percent; in 1958, 38 percent; and in 1968, the figure was reported to have dropped to 22 percent.[29] This means that men,

29. John Hoyle, "Who Shall Be Principal—A Man or A Woman?" *The National Elementary Principal*, no. 3 (January, 1969), pp. 23–25.

who constitute only 12 percent of the teaching force in elementary schools, hold 78 percent of the elementary principalships!

How did this happen? Obviously, superintendents and boards of education think that men are more capable administrators. The boards, incidentally, are heavily male-dominated and the superintendents of large school districts almost exclusively male.[30] Do their choices reflect a reasoned and informed judgment as to who makes the best principal? Or is this yet another case of sex bias gone rampant?

Reviewing recent research findings as to what qualities and characteristics are required for principals to be effective, Hoyle suggests that there are no reasons for preferring men. In fact, women rate better than men as "democratic leaders" and in administrative skills. It was not true, moreover, that teachers prefer male principals. They rated them about equally. One authoritative study by Kenneth McIntyre concluded that ". . . research does not show men to be superior to women in the principalship—in fact, the little evidence we have suggests just the opposite conclusion." [31]

To clinch the argument, it should be pointed out that the record shows men were appointed as principals with less teaching experience than their female colleagues who came to be so honored. Of the males, 66.7 percent had *less* than six years of teaching experience at the time of their advancement. Conversely, 88 percent of the female principals had *more* than six years of teaching experience when they started their jobs.

Sex discrimination in education is, of course, of tremendous importance for the opportunities and advances of women into any field, and we shall discuss it fully at some later point. What has been shown so far is that in the profession women have moved into in the greatest number, the social mobility offered them is severely limited. The powers that be in education, heavily male in composition at all

30. In Minnesota, for example, it was found that there were *no* female superintendents of schools.

31. Kenneth E. McIntyre, "The Selection of Elementary School Principals," quoted in Hoyle, "Who Shall Be Principal?"

levels, give pronounced preferential treatment to men. Women, again, have to take the back seat.

Library work is another profession dominated by women. In 1968, 95,000 women were employed in this category, and made up about 90 percent of all librarians. What does the status of the sexual majority in this profession reveal about the social mobility of women?

The first fact to stare us in the face is this: Here, too, women have suffered a decline in status that is quite drastic. In an article entitled "The Widening Sex Gap," Anita R. Schiller points out that in 1930 women had 19 and men 55 of the chief librarianships in 74 large colleges and universities. A check of the same positions in these libraries today reveals that only 4 of them are held by women and 70 by men. Among academic librarians, specifically, there are nearly twice as many women as men. Yet not one of the largest academic libraries in the United States is headed by a woman.[32]

Salary differentials for men and women in this profession are also striking. For one thing, the median yearly salary for men is $8,990 and for women $7,455—about $1,500 less. In spite of the far greater numbers of women librarians, we find that the proportion of men in higher positions is much higher than that of women. The chance for a woman to become a head librarian is only about half as good as the chance of a man. The libraries women get to administer are also generally smaller and the salaries lower. Thus among chief librarians, the median yearly salary for men is $11,700, while for women it is only $8,300. Men who are *not* chief librarians tend to do as well as or better than women who *are*. The gap cannot be ascribed to differences in educational level or experience between the sexes. Anita R. Schiller points out that women with the *same* amount of professional experience and education as men are compensated at a *lower* rate. The more experience they acquire, the greater their disadvantage. The data available show very clearly that in this profession, too, "women are the underprivileged majority." Although they are freely accepted into its ranks, their future advancement in the profession is limited.

32. Anita R. Schiller, "The Widening Sex Gap," *Library Journal* (March 15, 1969), pp. 1097–1101.

We have, then, proof of yet another case of restricted social mobility for women. Others can be brought up, so many others that the exploration could easily become tedious. The professions we have concerned ourselves with here are of central importance because they are among the very few that women have made inroads into and even come to dominate in numbers. Also, because salaries and ranks and advancements in these professions are supposedly determined by educational attainment, experience, and demonstrated ability, and no other considerations, the bias introduced is illegitimate, if not illegal. When we find it operating as we have to the serious detriment of hundreds of thousands of women professionals, we can only draw the conclusion that if there is a sex gap in *these* fields of endeavor, it is a reflection of a bias that is as pervasive as it is deeply embedded in American institutions. In income and in social mobility, working women have been shown to be so severely disadvantaged that one suspects social forces in operation that are as yet beyond the grasp and influence of most of us.

Three

INSTITUTIONAL SEXISM

"Sex prejudice," in the words of poet Eve Merriam, "is the only prejudice now considered socially acceptable.[1]

To that, any number of women seeking equal opportunities in higher education and on the job market are likely to say "Amen"! What is remarkable about the sex bias operative in these fields is not just that it is so widespread, but that it is very often frankly expressed. Story after story is passed around among women telling of the semi-comic and yet revolting prejudices expressed by male bosses, colleagues, and professors. For that matter, women themselves can be quite expert at denigrating their own sex. Although an educated, progressive man—or woman—would think twice, to say the least, before talking about someone of a different race being unfit for certain jobs, having less of a potential for development, and also having less of a "need" for advancement and higher income, that same person will not hesitate to say *exactly* that and *more* of a woman.

Typical of the comments by male employers are the following: "Your qualifications for this job seem just fine, but we just don't hire women in this category." It can be put more bluntly, of course: "This field is not for women." "Women don't fit in here." "You may be an exception, but women are generally too emotional and un-

1. Quoted in Cynthia Fuchs Epstein, *Women's Place* (Berkeley: University of California Press, 1970), p. 34.

reliable under stress to handle this kind of job." "Can you type instead?"

Even President Nixon's Labor Secretary, James D. Hodgson, has publicly recognized the profound sex bias in the labor market. Job discrimination against women, declared Hodgson in the summer of 1970, is "more subtle and more pervasive than against any other minority group." [2]

This sobering conclusion is given support by prominent Negro women. Many report, as did Congresswoman Shirley Chisholm and lawyer Pauli Murray, that in their lives they have experienced far more discrimination on the grounds of sex than of race. [3] A frank management consultant, quoted by Caroline Bird, typifies this common attitude: In response to a job query by a woman executive, he confessed, "I'm not ready for a woman. But, boy, would I love to get hold of a good Negro!" [4]

The parallels in attitudes towards women and blacks in America have been noted by expert observers like Gunnar Myrdal and Helen Hacker. Both groups are held to be "childlike," inferior in intelligence, emotional, and incapable of genius. Both are said to be "all right in their places" and to really prefer staying there. They—women and blacks—are also recognized as being typically capable of deviousness, intrigue, and intuitive powers. Those of both groups who accept their role in life without complaint are the "good" Negroes or the "real" women, and those who want change are "uppity" or "sick." The stock response to those who complain about their roles is: "What do you want—to be white?" or "What do you want—to be a man?"

Shirley Chisholm has recently given testimony to the persistence of these attitudes:

> To keep them in their place, the same characteristics are imputed
> to women as to blacks—that they are more childish, emotional and

2. Quoted in the *San Francisco Chronicle*, July 26, 1970, "Magazine" section, p. 7.

3. Alice C. Rossi, "Job Discrimination and What Women Can Do about It," *Atlantic Monthly*, March, 1970, pp. 99–103.

4. Caroline Bird, *Born Female* (New York: Pocket Books, 1969), p. 125.

irresponsible than men, that they are of lower intelligence than men, that they need protection, that they are happiest in routine, undemanding jobs, and that they lack ambition and executive ability.[5]

Of late, one difference has been introduced. With the success of the civil rights movement in removing legal barriers against full equality for blacks and in getting the media's attention and sympathy for their cause, it has at long last become unacceptable—or, at the very least, unfashionable©to express racial prejudice. Not so, however, with prejudice against women.

It used to be said that blacks "are the last to be hired, the first to be fired." That situation seems to have changed, at the very least in the academic and professional fields that can most easily catch the spotlight and become the target of demonstrations and protests. Today, if not in the past, it is women who are the last to be hired and the first to be fired.

More revealing data comes our way through an examination of both unemployment characteristics and cases of job discrimination filed before the equal Employment Opportunities Commission (EEOC). As to the latter, we find that in the area of hiring, complaints by women exceeded those of men by a ratio of four to one. And as to unemployment, the rate for women in 1969 was double that of men, 4.7 percent to 2.8 percent.[6] Among black citizens, the unemployment rates for men have been reduced significantly from a high of 12.8 percent in 1961 to 5.6 percent in 1968. But for black women the drop is less sharp, from 11.8 percent to a still drastic 8.3 percent. To discover who are the first to be fired today, we have to look specifically at the rate of *job losers* as against *job leavers*. Here we find that the rate of job losers is almost *three times* that of job leavers in the unemployment figures for women. Quite simply, women are fired more frequently than men, losing their jobs at a rate of 3.8 percent as against 2.2 percent for men.[7]

5. Testimony before a House subcommittee considering legislation opposing discrimination against women. Quoted in *The Militant,* July 17, 1970, p. 18.
6. Rossi, "Job Discrimination," p. 101.
7. *The 1969 Handbook on Women Workers,* pp. 67–69.

"You can't make that demand. We haven't even conceded it to blacks yet!" was the response of a council member of the American Psychological Association to a request by women professionals in 1969 that accreditation be withheld from departments that cannot show nondiscrimination. The point made was quickly noted by one shocked female psychologist: "This just shows that women are even a second-class minority group. We can only ask for what blacks have already got." [8]

I.

What all of this points to is that women are suffering from a phenomenon closely akin to *racism*. That term has come to mean a system of social, political, and psychological pressures that tends to suppress a group with certain biologically determined characteristics. To prove the existence of racism, it must be shown that the suppression goes beyond or is contrary to normal divisions of class. A black unskilled laborer may be suppressed and exploited, but it is a case of racist oppression only if his vulnerability and suffering is greater than is that of his white co-worker. As a black, he must be shown to have been made a member of a class within a class. A victim of racism will thus be systematically relegated to a substrata within the major strata he or she belongs to by occupation and educational achievement.

This seems to be precisely the system in operation in regard to women on the labor market. If anything, the suppression of women is even more systematic and severe, although a great deal more subtle, than that of black men. At the same time, it must be recognized that there *are* avenues of escape open to women that are pretty much foreclosed to other minority members.[9] Marriage still is foremost

8. Quoted in Jo Freeman, "The Revolution Is Happening in Our Minds," *College and University Business,* February, 1970, p. 67.

9. We use the term "minority" here as a sociological and not a statistical concept, the identifying factor being the presence of discrimination against group members.

among these, although its value as an "escape," as noted, has been severely diminished with the greatly increased impermanency of the institution.

It must also be recognized that in the female group, it is *black* women who suffer the most (with the possible exception of Indian women). They have to carry on their backs the double burden of being black and being female in a society where both identities carry with them distinct and serious disadvantages. How staggering that burden can be is indicated by the fact that among all major groups in our society, poverty is *most likely* to hit a nonwhite family headed by a woman. In 1965, for example, a full 62 percent of these families, 1,132,000 in number, were poor.[10]

Yet in comparing median salaries of men and women, black and white, and in surveying the social and economic situation confronting each sex, it seems clear that black women have as much, if not more, of a common cause with their white sisters on the job market as they do with their black brothers. It is women who turn out to be the "niggers" in virtually every job category. It is working women who are made to carry the heaviest social burden—the bearing and rearing of children, the cooking and housework "after hours," and the major job of providing for the family when a husband is no longer on the scene. It is well worth re-emphasizing the following data: Women who are heads of their families must on the average contribute by themselves nearly three-fourths (72 percent) of the family's income.[11] And housewives with only part-time jobs average a 68-hour work week, combining housework and outside labor. Husbands, on the other hand, have their 40-hour week plus only *fifteen minutes a day* to help out with children and housework.[12]

"Woman As Nigger" is, indeed, the title of a provocative article by Gayle Rubin. In it, she points out that "people are more sophisticated about blacks than they are about women: black history courses do not have to begin by convincing people that blacks are

10. U.S. Department of Labor, Wage and Labor Standards Administration, *Negro Women—In the Population and in the Labor Force* (December, 1967).
11. Robert L. Stein, "Women At Work," *Monthly Labor Review* (June, 1970).
12. According to a study of housewives in Syracuse, N.Y., quoted in *Sheryn's Nifty Newsletter*, I, no. 1 (May, 1970), p. 2.

not in fact genetically better suited to dancing than to learning." [13]
That women are capable of different roles is still not recognized.
Notably, the word "sex" was included in the 1964 Civil Rights Act
as a joke. Miss Rubin reminds us that it was opposed by all liberals
on the ground that it would make the whole Civil Rights Act more
difficult to pass!

The racism we are discussing here, most aptly referred to as *sexism*,
is not just a phenomenon in the minds of men and women in America. To the extent that it exists, it is, as are all systems that maintain
relationships of dominance and subordination, *institutionalized*. It
also has an *ideology*, implanted and perpetrated by institutions centrally located in the political socialization process. Last but not
least, it has an *interest structure* that provides the underlying ra-
tionale and dynamic for the ongoing process.

II.

Controls and discriminatory patterns affecting any group are always maintained through legal codes and/or institutionalized behavior so well entrenched that the persons involved often are not
conscious of operating in a racist manner. In a democracy, one
sooner or later has to conform with the basic principle of equality
under the law, and it is thus mainly the institutional web that up-
holds racist patterns of behavior. Strikingly, in comparing the status
and rights of women and black men in our society, we find—again
—that it is women who have had to take the back seats when it
comes to the elimination of legal codes sanctifying discrimination.

There is, in the first place, the obvious and glaring omission of
women from the Fourteenth and Fifteenth Amendments. Sex was
left out of both: voting rights and equality of rights under the law
were guaranteed to all citizens without regard to race, creed, or
color—as long as they were male. It took more than half a century

13. Gayle Rubin, "Woman As Nigger," *The Argus*, March 28–April 11, 1970,
pp. 7–15. The passage quoted appears on p. 7.

of bitter struggle to win for women the first and most basic right in a democracy—a right that minority males were formally accorded in 1867. The rights guaranteed by the Fifteenth Amendment to all men in our society—a century after its passage—are still not extended to women. The fight to get passage of the disputed Twenty-sixth Amendment, "The Women's Amendment," met with some success at last in the summer of 1970, when the 47-year-old proposal passed the House by an overwhelming vote of 350 to 15. Senate approval and ratification by 38 states is still needed, however, and will, needless to say, take years longer. All the amendment proposes, incidentally, is that "equality of rights under the law shall not be denied and abridged by the United States or by any state on account of sex." Elementary enough, it would seem.

The opposition to the amendment was led by Congressman Emanuel Celler (Dem. √—N.Y.). His comments, though quaint, reflect attitudes still common both in the legal profession and in the population at large: "There is more difference between a man and a woman than between a horse chestnut and a chestnut horse," declared the aging but powerful chairman of the House Judiciary Committee as he dismissed the "blunderbuss" amendment.[14]

As late as 1908, the Supreme Court itself was quite explicit in its assertion of female inferiority. Said the illustrious Court: ". . . History discloses the fact that woman has always been dependent upon man. . . . Looking at it from the viewpoint of the effort to maintain an independent position in life . . . she is properly placed in a class by herself." [15] The opinion of the Court in this instance was right in line with its earlier decision in the 1872 case of *Bradwell* vs. *Illinois*. Here, a woman was refused permission to practise law on the grounds that it was the law of the Creator that ". . . the paramount destiny and mission of women are to fulfill the noble and benign offices of wife and mother." [16]

14. *San Francisco Chronicle,* August 16, 1970, p. 7.
15. Quoted in Diane Schulder, "Women and the Law," *Atlantic Monthly,* March, 1970, pp. 103–5.
16. Barbara Bates Gunderson, "The Implication of Rivalry," in Seymour M. Farber and Roger H. L. Wilson, eds., *The Potential of Woman* (New York: McGraw-Hill Book Co., 1963), pp. 165–85.

It must be admitted that we have come *some* way since then. At the same time, it is worth noting that this most brave and persistent of our institutions in the defense of democratic ideals *as late as 1970* still had not found it possible to deal with certain specific injustices against the female half of the nation. It has, by and large, reaffirmed the "protective" approach towards women. In 1948, for example, the Supreme Court upheld the right of states to refuse a woman the right to become a bartender unless she was "the wife or daughter of the male owner." The Court explained:

> The fact that women now have achieved the virtues that men have long claimed as their prerogatives and now indulge in vices that men now practise, does not preclude the States from drawing a sharp line between the sexes, certainly in such matters as the regulation of liquor traffic. The Constitution does not require legislatures to reflect sociological insight or shifting social standards.[17]

That—only a few years prior to the monumental segregation decision, *Brown* vs. *Board of Education,* which, *drawing on sociological insight,* concluded that segregation by race in public schools is by its very nature unequal and therefore unconstitutional, thereby setting new and different social standards for a whole nation!

Other omissions by the Court in regard to women (as of mid-1970) include women's exclusion from juries, leaving a wife's earnings in control of her husband (in four states), and labor laws which prevent women from working overtime, lifting weights, and the like.

In the labor market generally, this last restriction has long been the principal legal barrier against the advancement of women into higher-paying positions. The Equal Pay Act, passed in 1963, and the Civil Rights Act, Title VII, passed the following year, open the way for legal protests against sex discrimination in most aspects of employment. But the "protective" legislation still in existence provides employers with a convenient excuse to keep women out of jobs with higher pay and status.

Working hours for women, for instance, are limited in 36 states; in 20 of these states women are expressly prohibited from working

17. Quoted in Schulder, "Women and the Law," p. 103.

more than 8 hours a day or 48 hours a week. They are thus protected from the opportunity of earning any substantial overtime pay—and from promotion to jobs requiring much overtime. Women are also prohibited from entering certain occupations and industries in 26 states—usually occupations and industries where the average pay is higher than that in job categories occupied by women. The suffocating paternalism of the law can be explicit, as it is in Michigan, where the code states: "No female shall be given any task disproportionate to her strength, nor shall she be employed in any place detrimental to her morals, her health, and her capacity for motherhood." [18]

This is not to say that there is a deliberate or consciously evolved conspiracy among male bosses and colleagues to prevent the advancement of women into more profitable fields. That such is the *effect* of the numerous objections and reservations raised concerning women's fitness or abilities for certain work is quite clear. But the effectiveness of sexism on the labor market depends on how well sexist differentiation and sexist controls operate in other institutional sectors. If, for instance, men and women alike can be convinced through the socialization process alone that woman's place is in the home and/or that women are less logically inclined and more emotionally unstable than men, then the sanctions of a legal framework may not be needed to maintain patterns of discrimination and control. As the authors of an illuminating work on institutional racism have made clear, discriminatory behavior has become so well institutionalized that individuals generally do not have to exercise a choice to operate in a racist manner. The choices have already been prestructured. The individual has only to conform to the operating norms of the organization he is involved with and the institution will do the discriminating for him.[19]

The techniques for keeping women down are nevertheless overt, far more so than those used to maintain white superiority. Take, for example, the specification for males in the "Help Wanted"

18. *Life* Magazine, September 4, 1950, p. 18.
19. Louis Knowles and Kenneth Prewitt, *Institutional Racism in America* (Englewood Cliffs, N.J.: Prentice-Hall, Inc., 1969), p. 142.

columns of publications today, which is illegal under Title VII of the Civil Rights Act. Any comparison of the jobs offered men with those offered women quickly makes obvious how severe is the opportunity gap between the sexes. Efforts to abolish this particular discrimination have so far proved useless; a challenge of the practice caused it to be abolished for a brief period in 1969, but it was then resumed in nearly all major publications on the grounds that it was the only practical way to advertise jobs. Consider, now, what would surely happen today if employers publicly specified "whites only" in the "Help Wanted" columns! Even in the Civil Service such flagrant violations of fair employment principles are quite common as far as women are concerned. A survey of the Civil Service Commission some years ago disclosed that 94 percent of the requests received from government agencies for top management jobs specified men.[20]

Just how gross and glaring the put-down of women on the *highest* official levels can be was unwittingly demonstrated by the White House in the fall of 1970. The occasion was a state dinner given by President Nixon for Mexican President Diaz Ordaz in San Diego. The 50 night-shift waitresses on duty at the Hotel del Coronado were plainly told by the hotel management that they wouldn't be needed for this auspicious event. In such grand company, the presence of male waiters was required, compliments of the White House. This one time, however, in a year of women's liberation ferment, the offense was not passed over lightly. Protests were lodged, letters poured in both from the waitresses and from women activists, and the White House hastened to change its plans and simply *add* 50 male waiters, maintaining the 50 female waitresses on duty as usual. Asked then why the word went out to hire only men for the additional help needed, the press secretary in charge explained that it was because "the manner in which you serve usually requires a male waiter trained to serve in this manner." This meant, she added, when further pressed, "serving by platter." [21] An operation

20. Adrienne Koch, "Two Cheers for Equality," in Farber and Wilson, *The Potential of Women*, p. 212.

21. *San Francisco Chronicle*, September 2, 1970, p. 5.

too complex and difficult for women? Only in the context of institutional sexism can such insensitivity on the part of the presidential office be comprehended. Consider the reaction if the original
50 had been black!

III.

The evidence so far indicates that woman's role in the economy
today is confined to that of employee and consumer. Women executives or women bosses, as a recent survey by the *Harvard Business Review* points out, are so few and far between that they might
as well be left out of the picture.[22] As for the much touted wealth
of American women, investigation shows it to be of minimal importance for the exertion of influence and control of business operations. We shall come back to this point in a later chapter; for now
it is enough to disclose that women constitute only one-third of
the top wealth-holders of this country, that they come by their
money late in life (one-third of them are widows), and that their
assets, besides being usually handled by male managers and executives, are by and large of the kind that are not easily converted
into cash for financial maneuvers.[23]

Exclusion from ownership and/or control of industry and business has far-reaching consequences for any group in our society.
For women, as for black men, it limits their strength and opportunities in many noneconomic areas of life. It is also, as the
authors of *Institutional Racism* point out, a major element in
defining the constraints of racism.[24] For a woman—as for a black
man—this means that we can best comprehend her basic role if
we consider her as a seller of labor in the job market. But for a
woman, we have to also consider her role as an *unsalaried* worker,
uncovered by any laws regulating either hours, benefits, or manner

22. Quoted in Epstein, *Woman's Place*, p. 6.
23. See Roger Lampman, *The Share of Top Wealth Holders in National
Wealth, 1956* (Princeton, N.J.: Princeton University Press, 1962).
24. Knowles and Prewitt, *Institutional Racism*, p. 146.

of work. Woman as a housewife is, in this sense, the most underprivileged of all laborers. That she may and often does share in
the income and prestige coming to her husband does not change
the fact that this award is meted out voluntarily. The housework
performed by her is not recognized as sufficiently socially useful to
require the governmental protection extended to other types of
labor. One might say that a housewife is equally a seller in the
job market. For her efforts she gets whatever marriage can offer—
with no guarantee of either salary, benefits, or tenure in office.

Our primary focus is still on the woman at work, but it must be
understood that the role of the housewife in the economy is in-
extricably tied to the role of the female employee. The sexual
dualism on the labor market is in no small measure due to the acceptance by women of the former role as an—or *the*—essential one.
The differently structured set of opportunities offered women are
defended on the basis of this ideology, at the same time that the
supply of women to the job market can be more easily expanded
and constricted because, presumably, women can always return to
"home base." New job opportunities for women come only during
periods of a tight labor market, when the pool of male labor is
drying up. Women then constitute a reserve labor force, to be used
if and when male employers, and not the workers themselves, find
it opportune.

It is in this, and only in this, sense that women workers are
marginal to the labor force. Their involvement and activities on
the job market are of central importance both to the women themselves and to the employers who engage their services. But a labor
boss can afford to be far more highhanded in dismissing women
than men. He can also send out calls for women to come in for seasonal work and keep them for just the "right" period to avoid pay-
ing for leaves, pensions, and other fringe benefits. And he can,
above all, justify the lower pay offered women on the basis that
women, after all, are not the family breadwinners. They just "don't
need" as much as men.

The major flaw in this proposition has already been exposed: we
have seen that the majority of women, at least 20 million in number,

work because of stark material, and not fancied or real psychological, need. But the *myth* holds sway and the economic structure continues to provide job earnings and opportunities in a vastly unequal manner for men and women. Sex consequently divides the job market into more distinct and different sectors than does race. A whole array of jobs are designated as women's jobs and these are almost without exception jobs that offer incomes below the median income of males. How strong and insidious the web of discrimination is can best be illustrated by a look at some of the major occupation groups of employed women over the last 30 years. In 1940, women made up 40.1 percent of service workers; in 1968, 57 percent; in 1940 women were 52.6 percent of clerical workers and 27.9 percent of sales workers; in 1968 the percentages of women in the same categories were 72.6 percent and 39.7 percent respectively. On the other hand, women's share of positions as technical and professional workers *deteriorated* in the same time span from 45.4 percent in 1940 to 38.6 percent in 1968.[25] What has happened is that as women have moved into the labor market in greater numbers, they have consistently been channeled into the lower-status occupations and to a great extent kept out of the higher-paid ones. The result is a deterioration of the position of working women in terms of their share of income, status, and social mobility in the last decades.

Sexism in the job market operates, then, basically in two ways: one, by confining women largely to the positions considered "suitable" for them, that is, the lesser-paid and lower-prestige positions; and two, by limiting women to specific job classifications and production units within the establishments that hire both men and women. Here, occupational ceilings are set for women in nearly every instance. For them to advance to positions of responsibility and leadership, it is necessary that they be "twice as good as men," as innumerable women have testified. Women are quite simply in a subordinate position and it seems that they are meant to stay there.

25. *The 1969 Handbook on Women Workers,* p. 92.

IV.

It stands to reason that someone does benefit. To say that society does is a misstatement as glaring as it is shallow. Societies are human constructs that *can* take a variety of forms and *should,* given our value system, take the form that offers the maximum number of people the maximum opportunities for a good life. Present arrangements may serve the dominant, that is, the prevailing interests of the present political system, but that does not mean that the majority of citizens are well served by them. If they are not, then no semi-religious adulation of society's needs can be allowed to stand in the way of change. A society is simply a complex of human interrelationships with certain distinct patterns and a fairly definite boundary. Either of these elements can be transformed, partially or wholly, and the democratic creed would hold that they should be transformed when they get in the way of desired change. Societies are for people, quite simply, and not the other way around.

So who actually benefits? Only as we discover the answer to this question can we name and deal with the interest structure that is at the basis of the economic exploitation of women. It is clear that women do not, neither the 31-odd million now on the labor market, the many millions more who would enter it if they had a chance, or the innumerable others who are going to have to enter it sporadically or permanently in the years ahead. Neither are the children of these women better off because of the practice of discrimination. The low pay, the long hours, the lack of fringe benefits (child-care centers foremost among them), all have the effect of making lives poorer, harder, and crueler, both for mothers and children. In 1968 4.5 million children lived in poverty because their mothers, the main supporters of the family, could not get a salary in their full-time jobs that would lift them above this level. Millions of others live in "near poverty" because of the same situation.

At this time, it is far too easy an answer to point an accusing finger at men in general, for clearly, the husbands, the fathers, the brothers, and the sons of working women have, at least, a *material* interest in seeing the women of the family lift themselves up from their presently sorry socioeconomic state. It is also difficult to imagine a closely related male deliberately striving to deprive a woman of higher earnings and status that would be due her were she a man. To wish her to stay home, to express doubts in her ability and hostility to her ambition is quite another thing. Such attitudes have been inculcated in men—and in women as well— through the socialization process. But confronted with a working woman in the family, is it likely that a man would *actively* wish and work for her taking a back seat to male colleagues performing the same job? It could happen—and it no doubt has. One should be allowed to assume, however, that a good number of American men do not have to cling so precariously to their male egos that they cannot accept equality of opportunity for female family members, especially since their own economic burdens might be significantly lessened with such an arrangement. An insight into this possibility should be enough, were their humanitarian impulse to fail them, for them to accept the change.

But the common man does not, of course, have much to do with decisions to hire or to fire, to raise wages, and to create benefits for workers, whether male or female. Sex prejudice is pervasive, yes, but that does not mean everyone is equally responsible for the sexist differentiations on the labor market. It is to those empowered to make decisions we must look when we want change—*and when we want to find out why it hasn't taken place.*

We have defined woman as a consumer and as a seller of labor in the present economic system. We have also pointed to her marginal position, in the sense that she constitutes the greatest reserve labor force available in our society. This is of central importance for the comprehension of the interest structure underlying the web of discrimination on the job market, for the use of women as temporary workers, full- or part-time, is one of the most profitable arrangements available to employers in contemporary times. It is also a device to prevent any serious reordering of present structures and to allow the economy to expand and contract in response to new opportunities for the business elites and *not* in response to the needs of workers.

Take first the *extra profits* coming to employers because of the temporary status of many women workers and the comparatively lower earnings of all of them. Fringe benefits today are quite costly to the owners of business enterprises. Vacation pay, sick leave, extra medical benefits, contributions to pension plans—all of these can be avoided if employees stay at their job for only part of the day or part of the year, say 90 days. This lesson has not been lost on the bosses of America. As economist Joan Jordan points out, it has become more and more common to maintain a skeleton crew of prime full-time workers, eliminating the young, the old, and the inexperienced women, and then to hire a supplementary crew of part-time workers.[26] Seasonal work is also increasing, as the time study men in corporations are discovering its economic benefits. Layoff early in November, for instance, avoids extra pay for Veterans Day, Thanksgiving, Christmas, Washington's and Lincoln's birthdays, and whatever other holidays the workers have won guarantees of. Extra medical benefits and, of course, vacation pay are avoided by hiring women for three months in the summer. By cavalierly dismissing women workers with the rationalization that they are not the main breadwinners anyway, employers have the advantage of maintaining a floating crew of experienced labor at cheap rates, without having to take on any of the responsibilities and expenses that come their way by the maintenance of a full, regularly employed crew.

Ironically enough, these exploitative maneuvers often have the assistance of local unions. It is through them that the temporary hiring and firing is usually done. The 90-day-or-less workers are asked to pay dues, too, under the illusion that they will be initiated into the union after a waiting period. But if they are laid off before initiation, they are not considered members and the dues are kept in the local, although the union has no obligation to

26. Joan Jordan, *The Place of American Women* (Boston: New England Free Press, 1969).

find them jobs. Quite a windfall, as Joan Jordan comments, for the union officer who is more concerned with dues than with grievances! [27] While it may appear to be a temporary gain for male union members in general, further reflection shows this to be a very shortsighted view. The use of women as a reserve labor force, just like the use of blacks for the same purpose, has the effect of making men more dispensable as well and of depressing wages for *all* groups on the grounds that if anyone prices himself out of the market, replacements can easily be found. Present union members' desperate clinging to their security and advantages, with little or no regard for newcomers to the labor force, not only has prevented the expansion of the union movement in the last decades, but has also proven to be of little avail to long-time unionists as the economy constricts at the behest of business elites. Support for and loyalty to fellow workers, of both sexes, *might,* on the other hand, have put labor in the position to prevent such constriction. Greater in numbers and more superior in unity, the union movement would be in a much stronger position to make its claims upon the economic system. It must be kept in mind, after all, that ours is a system where scarcity of resources is no longer a basic problem; the question now is one of priorities for spending and not one of finding the economic means with which to keep everyone at work.[28]

The advantage, if any, to male union members of maintaining women workers in their present situation is at best of short duration and carries with it serious long-term costs. But to employers, the case for discrimination can be made easily enough. *The savings made possible by keeping women as a reserve labor force, although considerable, are as nothing compared to the profits to be had by continuing the lower wages offered women for work identical to that performed by men.* Some employers are even honest about it, reveals Lyn Wells. One of them replied, during the Conference on Equal Pay in 1952, when asked why the pay of women in his factory

27. Ibid., p. 5.
28. See, for example, J. K. Galbraith's analysis in *The Affluent Society* (Boston: Houghton Mifflin Co., 1958).

was less than that of men: "Tradition, I suppose, . . . anyhow, it's cheaper." [29]

Exactly how much cheaper the arrangement may be is suggested in a study by Grace Hutchins. Using 1950 Census reports and figures from the Securities and Exchange Commission, she calculates that in 1950 manufacturing companies realized profits of $5.4 billion by paying women less per year than the wages paid to men for similar work.[30] The extra profits extracted in this way formed 23 percent of all company profits that year.[31] Although an Equal Pay Act requiring equal pay for equal work has been in existence since 1963, violations are still frequent and serious. The Wage and Hours Division of the Department of Labor has, in fact, found that by April, 1970, over $17 million in underpayments were owed to more than 50,000 employees, nearly all of them women.[32]

To know *where* women work is also of importance for the full comprehension of the interest structure maintained by their subjugation. Industries that are highly automated and enjoy nearly monopolistic control in their area of production have less of a need to control wages than do industries that are labor-intensive. In the former, higher wages are simply passed on to the consumer in the form of higher prices—with no effective government controls, labor costs are not allowed to affect profits. But in industries with low rates of automation, such as the textile and clothing industries, substantially higher wages would mean not just less profit but a transformation or demise of the enterprise. In textiles, for instance, it might force automation, if the industry is to survive the competition from abroad. How this bears on the problem of women is brilliantly shown by Peggy Morton. The industries with the lowest rate of automation are also those who employ the greater num-

29. Lyn Wells, *American Women—Their Use and Abuse* (Boston: New England Free Press, 1969), p. 9.

30. Grace Hutchins, *Women Who Work* (New York: International Publishers, 1952), p. 12.

31. Jordan, *The Place of American Women*, p. 16.

32. Robert L. Stein, "Women At Work," *Monthly Labor Review* (June, 1970), p. 32.

ber of women. About 70 percent of women workers are in the textile, clothing, and related industries, in food and beverages, or in electrical appliances or supplies. How crucial are the savings to be had from the lower wages paid women is amply illustrated by a comparison of average weekly wages in 1969: For clothing and related industries, where women workers dominate, they were $78 and in leather products $81; whereas in chemicals and nonmetallic leather products, where women make up only 22 percent and 11 percent of the workers respectively, the wages were $139 and $133.[33]

But more women are, of course, employed in the service sector than in manufacturing. Work here is most often uncreative and tedious, working conditions are bad, and economic rewards are minimal. A good part of the women here belong to the "economic underworld," as Michael Harrington aptly names it,[34] financially backward, immune to progress, incredibly capable of being exploited. Unions are kept out, by and large, and when allowed in, it is the labor racketeers who are invited to make deals without any of the standard provisions for wage rates, fringe benefits, and so forth, of honest union contracts. The shortsightedness of labor leaders is again to be blamed: it is the AFL-CIO "No Raiding" agreement that makes this possible. Once a racket local has a charter in a recognized international, honest unions are stopped from going in to take over from the crooks. And again, the arrangement causes more women than men to suffer. Unions have been notably lax in extending their protection to women: only one out of seven women workers belongs to a union; for men the ratio is one out of four.

Wages in the economic underworld reflect the unprotected state of women workers. Chambermaids in hotels got only $1.25 in average hourly wages in 1967, hotel waitresses only $.95. In laundry and cleaning services, where women constituted slightly more than three-fourths of the nonsupervisory personnel, the average earnings

33. Peggy Morton, "A Woman's Work Is Never Done," *Leviathan*, II, no. 1 (May, 1970), pp. 32-38.
34. Michael Harrington, *The Other America* (New York: The Macmillan Company, 1963), p. 26.

were $1.56 per hour in 1968. Conditions are similar among service workers in hospitals—also mainly women.[35]

It stands to reason that *such low wages could not easily be offered to major groups of male workers today.* Neither is it likely that legislators on both federal and state levels would persist in their resistance to extend coverage of the minimum wage laws to such occupations were the workers affected mainly men. If millions of men rather than millions of women had to endure the low salaries and unprotected status of these professions, there would soon enough be grumblings, protests, organization, and strikes. But women are different, aren't they? Nonaggressive, nonambitious, preferring really to be homemakers, they also do not need to earn as much as men. Or so it is believed.

Only the secondary status of women in American society and their exclusion from the major centers of power could make possible such continued and severe exploitation of a major portion of the labor force. Those who benefit are, as has been shown, the business elites and no others.

35. *The 1969 Handbook on Women Workers,* pp. 155–57.

Four

POWER AND
THE AMERICAN WOMAN

The racism analogy holds up exceedingly well when applied to the problems of women on the job market. Women do indeed constitute a minority in the sociological sense, the largest and yet most exploited of all minorities in the labor force. It will no longer do, as has been pointed out, to rationalize the sex gap by insisting that women are basically homemakers. Like it or not, 31.1 million of them are wage-earners, 6.5 million self-supporting, and 5.6 million providing for their families as well. For the rest, work is often an economic necessity because of the low incomes of their husbands, not to speak of the instability of the institution of marriage. In spite of the fact that women, in Helen Hacker's ironic comment, are the only minority in history that lives with the master race,[1] it makes sense to define the position of women employees in the stratification system separately from the positions of their husbands or fathers. And when we do, it becomes clear that by far the majority of women working today belong with the working class in terms of salaries, benefits, and opportunities enjoyed.

As a working-class minority, women do, however, have possession of one resource that has the potential for power inherent in it, especially given the number of individuals involved here. That resource is *political*—citizenship or full membership in the political

1. Helen Hacker, "Women as a Minority Group," *Social Forces*, no. 3 (1951), p. 7.

class. Were it not for this important right, shared equally with men, working women might be most accurately designated as an "under" class, "a group without influence, subject to manipulation, and without legitimate means for redressing grievances." [2] The first two parts of the definition certainly fit. But then, women *do* have the vote. And the vote does, in fact, give them more than a "legitimate means" for redressing grievances; it provides them with a potential power base of great significance, given their superior numbers both in the nation and in the voting populace, for women constituted no less than 53.3 percent of eligible voters as of July, 1970.[3]

Citizenship is the one resource that—in a democracy—is equally distributed. It does not divide the nation into "have's" and "have not's." It can, quite to the contrary, be used by the latter to change the relationships in the distribution of goods and services in a society, for it is government that is the central agency for the authoritative allocation of resources and it is by effective use of the vote that a group or a coalition of groups can capture whole or partial control of the governmental machinery. Democracy's advantage and attractiveness as a governmental system stems in large part from its potential in this area. The one resource shared equally by all adult members of the society *may* be used by the socially and economically underprivileged to upset the status quo and to change the distributive pattern in existence at any time. The tables can be turned in the conflict between the "have's" and "have not's" when—and only when—the government becomes involved on behalf of those disadvantaged. *Numbers,* translated into *votes,* make the difference—numbers sufficient to put in office those who will act on behalf of groups of citizens exercising their democratic prerogative. Women are not only on a par with, they have it over, men in terms of *potential* for obtaining political power. *Why* is it, then, that their resources in this important sphere have not been translated into rights and benefits so sorely lacking for working women?

Equal pay, job opportunities, social security, employment in-

2. Louis Knowles and Kenneth Prewitt, *Institutional Racism in America* (Englewood Cliffs, N.J.: Prentice-Hall, Inc., 1969), p. 165.
3. *Congressional Record,* July 10, 1970, p. 1745.

surance, and other benefits are but some of the issues of great significance to citizens in a weak socioeconomic position. In the past
it is to government that they have turned, nearly all of them, to
get their due or to obtain the rights necessary to seek satisfaction
for their needs. Every impoverished and subordinated group in
America tends to follow this course of action, be it the small farm-
ers, the laborers, the blacks, or the farm workers. Invariably, their
fight to gain a greater measure of justice comes to focus on the need
to get the government on their side. Consider what the social land-
scape in America might be without the limit on working hours,
without social security, without the Wagner Act, without the minimum wage, or without civil rights legislation. It is certain that it
would be a different scene and it is probable that it would be a
much uglier one!

So what happened in regard to women? For more than half a
century now women have enjoyed formal political rights on an
equal basis with men. It is clear that this formidable weapon, full
membership in the political class, has been of little or no use to
this majority in terms of gaining equal rights and opportunities for
the 44 percent of it now in the labor force. Even if one were to
hypothesize a dichotomy of interests between women who work and
women who don't work, the sheer numbers of the former, 31.1
million as of 1970, would be quite enough to make a tremendous
political impact on legislation and rule-making in a system characterized by group politics—provided, of course, that they are *seen*
as an actual or potential group by the present lawmakers and provided that they, *as a group,* have representation in legislative councils and governmental agencies. But *that,* of course, entails something more than and different from a right to vote.

We have come to recognize, in viewing the struggle of blacks to
gain their share of the American pie, that the mere possession of
citizenship means precious little indeed for those left out of the
mainstream. Blacks have been able to vote not just for a half, but
for a whole century and are still intensely involved in the fight to
translate this essential resource into calculable and concrete social
advantages. In the process, they have had to go through several dis-

tinct stages of legal action, of extra-legal political activity, of self-exploration, of gaining recognition—all with the ultimate aim of organizing a political power base. The vote has to be used, first of all. The voters have to be unified on the crucial issues, pressure has to be applied on decision-makers at all levels, representatives have to be found to articulate and push through the demands of black citizens. Without such a power base, without representatives on the decision-making levels within political institutions, citizenship remains but a potential and not an actual resource for groups that are socially and economically disadvantaged.[4] The focus in the civil rights movement is increasingly on electing representatives to legislative bodies and seeking top administrative positions for individuals who can be relied on to act in the interest of the black minority. That such individuals might be nonblack is a possibility that is still disputed in the black community. What is uniformly recognized, however, is that black citizens are likely to gain a fairer and more effective representation if they capture for their own group members the maximum possible share of decision-making posts. To "get one's own people up there" is a desire that is as familiar as it is rational in societies where public representatives are entrusted with the authoritative allocation of scarce resources.

With this in mind, let us then take a realistic look at the political power base possessed by women in this country. They have the vote —OK. But of what use has it been up to now? What, for instance, is women's share of positions in legislatures, on top administrative levels, in city councils, on boards of supervisors and boards of education—in any and all of the institutions where membership presumably opens the way for equal and/or effective representation? Is their part of political power in these very real terms as negligible as the advances made by women in the occupational field? If so, then the latter situation is at least partially explained.

We shall, for the moment, proceed in this investigation on the

4. This has been most convincingly demonstrated in the works of T. H. Marshall, the British sociologist, for example, *Citizenship and Social Class* (London: Cambridge University Press, 1950), and by E. E. Schaltschneider, American political scientist, in *The Semi-Sovereign People* (New York: Holt, Rinehart and Winston, 1960).

assumption that there is a politically significant relationship between the proportion of representative positions a group can claim
for itself and the degree to which the needs and interests of that
group are articulated and acted upon in political institutions.[5] That
the relationship is not exact is evident enough: the proportion of
workers elected to or selected to decision-making positions in government is shockingly low, yet much legislation and rule making
benefitting workers has come through in recent decades.[6] It is clear,
on the other hand, that the continued social and economic privileges of the business and professional class are in no small measure
due to their striking overrepresentation in legislative councils. In
societies where members of the working class have captured for
themselves a fairer proportion of decision-making positions, the degree of social and economic inequality has been significantly reduced.

How do women fare, then? Are they to be found on the very
bottom of the stratification system in terms of this resource—political power—just as they are in regard to the other vital resources
already examined?

5. The concept of representation is as complex as it is elusive. It should be
made clear that I accept the definition offered by Hanna Pitkin that representation means acting in the interest of the represented, in a manner responsive to
them. See Hanna T. Pitkin, *The Concept of Representation* (Berkeley: University
of California Press, 1967), p. 209. This interpretation does not *require* that a
representative of a group be a member by birth, religion, or class affiliation of
the same group. It is considered likely, however, that the more group members
are in decision-making positions, the better chance the group has of fair
and effective representation.

For a provocative exploration into the meaning of representation to democratic governance, see also Heinz Eulau and Kenneth Prewitt, "Political Matrix
and Political Representation: Prolegomenon to a New Departure from an Old
Problem," *The American Political Science Review*, LXIII, no. 2 (June, 1969),
427–42.

6. In the period 1947–57 skilled and unskilled labor had only two representatives in Congress. In fact, government officials generally are recruited from the
well-educated and affluent upper and upper-middle classes. See Donald Matthews,
Social Background of Political Decision Makers (New York: Doubleday & Co.,
1954). See also U.S. Bureau of the Census, *Historical Statistics of the U.S.* (Washington, D.C.: Government Printing Office, 1962).

I.

We can start by looking at women's share of elective and appointive positions in the federal government.

The central position of the presidency in the American power structure is recognized by all scholars in the field. Yet none has cared to speculate on the anomaly that not one representative of the feminine half of the citizenry has been seriously considered for this all-important office. Worse than that, suggestions for a woman vice-president are brushed aside as flimsy, outrageous, embarrassing, or just amusing. The most serious of the few woman contenders for a vice-presidential nomination in the half-century since women got the vote, Senator Margaret Chase Smith, watched her fellow Republican policy-makers make short shrift of her campaign in the summer of 1968. And that in spite of the fact that she is one of the most respected and reliable vote-getters of her party.

Even to the most liberal of politicians the idea of a woman vice-president is apparently a far-out proposal. The late Robert Kennedy expressed some satisfaction several years ago in the possibility of seeing a woman in that merely potentially important office before the end of this century! [7]

It is notable, too, that there is today a greater acceptance of the possibility of having a black man as president than a woman. In 1969, only 54 percent of the electorate said they would be willing to vote for a woman for president, if a generally well-qualified woman were nominated by the party of preference. But 67 percent would be willing to vote for a black man in the same circumstances.[8] In other words, the black male minority, constituting no more than 5 percent of the nation, is considered to have more right of access to this most important of all political offices than the female half of this nation.

As we look at representatives in Congress, we find evidence of the same unexpected prejudice. In 1969–70 there were 11 black members

7. *Sacramento Bee,* April 14, 1967, p. 5.
8. *Gallup Opinion Index,* April, 1969, Report 46.

in the House of Representatives and only 10 women—10 among 435 members in all. In the Senate, with 100 members, each group is conceded 1 spokesman. If we were to have women representatives in these legislative bodies in accordance with the number of eligible women voters, there would be something like 220 congresswomen to 217 congressmen and 51 women senators to 49 men senators. Women, then, have 4 percent of the representation that is their due in the House—given a strictly mathematical interpretation of the concept.

In the Senate they fare even worse. Their representation there is only 2 percent of what it should be in proportion to their numbers in the population at large. By comparison, black citizens have by now achieved 30 percent of the representatives they are entitled to in the House and 10 percent in the Senate. Strikingly, the limited representation of blacks in these crucially important institutions is frequently—and rightfully—deplored, while the virtual absence of representation for women is given nary a mention!

The record of success for women politicians on this level was just about as dismal in the past as it is in the present. In the half-century since women have had the vote, only 65 women have won entrance to the House of Representatives and only 10 to the Senate. That makes for a 2 percent representation for women in Congress in the past 50 years. It is also worth noting that almost a majority of this special minority were given access to the lofty halls of Congress mainly because they happened to be widows of successful office-holders. Their parties offered them the nomination not out of a desire to open up the field to women, but in order to capitalize on the good will generated by the late husband, to gain the sympathy vote, or to prevent a general contest for office. As Martin Gruberg points out, before the highly successful and glamorous Claire Booth Luce was elected to office in 1942, almost all the female legislators had been either single or widows.[9]

But the political power of representatives has to be measured by other criteria than the mere holding of office. The ability to initiate

9. Martin Gruberg, *Women in Politics: A Source Book* (New York: Academic Press, 1968), p. 121.

and to amend legislation, the right and opportunity to take part in the investigative function of Congress, the influence over budget appropriations, the ability, ultimately, to give legislative help to one's constituents—all of this depends on the representative's committee assignments. The power hierarchy within both houses, supported by protocol, the committee and seniority systems, and the "informal folk-ways" of Washington, totally dominates the legislative arena. Without assignment to one of the prestigious committees and the ear and/or sympathy, if not the possession, of the chairmanship, the power of an individual member of Congress is significantly reduced. And if, in addition to the lack of "juicy" committee assignments, a representative does not gain access to and inclusion in the tangled web of informal and semi-structured relationships of power-wielders and influentials, he or she might as well forget about leaving an imprint on the legislation coming out of the nation's capital.

How do women representatives in Congress measure up when judged in terms of these criteria of power? The answer reveals itself easily enough as we examine their terms in office, their committee assignments, and their inclusion in the informal small groups of congressional leaders and intimates.

First, let us look at women's longevity in congressional offices. A freshman representative, it is customarily admitted, is unlikely to exercise any influence over public policy. Congressman Everett G. Burkhalter of California offered a succinct and revealing commentary on the situation in 1964. Explaining why he did not seek re-election, the 67-year-old representative said: "I could see I was not going to get any place. Nobody listens to what you have to say until you have been there 10 or 12 years. These old men have everything so tied down you can't do anything. There are only about 40 out of the 435 members who call the shots. They're the committee chairmen and the ranking members and they're all around 70 or 80." [10]

Of the 65 women who had served in Congress up to 1968, *24*

10. Quoted in Thomas R. Dye and L. Harmon Zeigler, *The Irony of Democracy* (Belmont, Calif.: The Wadsworth Publishing Co., Inc., 1970), p. 247.

stayed at the job *no more than one term or less.* Another 16 served two terms, and another 7 three. Only 22 Congresswomen in the last 50 years have been in office four or more terms—and it is widely accepted that it is not until the fourth term—and sometimes later —that a representative gains the recognition and influence among his peers that she or he needs to be an effective legislator.

Among the ten women Senators offered as proof that women have "made it" politically in the half-century the vote has been theirs, all of seven served less than one year! This is partly explained by the interesting fact that only five of the ten were elected to office. The lone woman hold-out in the world's most exclusive club, Senator Margaret Chase Smith, is now serving her sixth term. She, too, gained initial access to the political arena by being married to a successful politician.[11]

What about committee assignments and chairmanships? As Professor Frieda Geblen points out, women representatives have, over the years, been assigned disproportionately to the lesser-status committees, although in the Eighty-Eighth Congress—with 11 women members—3 made it into the most exclusive committees.[12] An authoritative chart of the congressional Establishment for the Ninety-First Congress reveals only 1 woman member among the 35 all-powerful individuals on the Hill. She is Margaret Chase Smith, who receives this designation by virtue of being named Republican Conference Chairman after five terms in office.[13]

The objective criteria for determining the position of women in the congressional power structure include also the election to party floor leadership and selection to the regional whip system, as conferees, or as chairmen. As to the first, women "do seem to be categorically eliminated from consideration at this time," concludes Professor Geblen, and in surveying the second, her caustic com-

11. Her husband was elected to Congress in 1937. When he was dying in 1937, he asked his constituents to elect his wife to fill out his term. Mrs. Smith won this and each subsequent election in which she was a candidate.

12. These are the Rules, Ways and Means, and Appropriation Committees. See Frieda Geblen, "Women in Congress," *Trans-action,* October, 1969, p. 37.

13. Dye and Zeigler, *The Irony of Democracy,* p. 249.

Table 4.1

THE CONGRESSIONAL ESTABLISHMENT FOR THE NINETY-FIRST CONGRESS, 1969–71

Senate Leadership

President pro tempore—Richard B. Russell (D–Ga.)
Majority Leader—Mike Mansfield (D–Mont.)
Majority Whip—Edward M. Kennedy (D–Mass.)
Democratic Conference Secretary—Robert C. Byrd (D–W.Va.)
Minority Leader—Everett McKinley Dirksen (R–Ill.)[1]
Minority Whip—Hugh Scott (R–Pa.)[2]
Republican Policy Committee Chairman—Gordon Allott (R–Colo.)
Republican Conference Chairman—Margaret Chase Smith (R–Maine)
Republican Conference Secretary—Milton R. Young (R–N.D.)

House Leadership

Speaker—John W. McCormack (D–Mass.)
Majority Leader—Carl Albert (D–Okla.)
Majority Whip—Hale Boggs (D–La.)
Minority Leader—Gerald R. Ford (R–Mich.)
Minority Whip—Leslie C. Arends (R–Ill.)
Republican Policy Committee Chairman—John J. Rhodes (R–Ariz.)
Republican Conference Chairman—John B. Anderson (R–Ill.)

Senate Committee Chairmen

Appropriations—Richard B. Russell (D–Ga.)
Armed Services—John Stennis (D–Miss.)
Labor and Public Welfare—Ralph Yarborough (D–Texas)
Banking and Currency—John J. Sparkman (D–Ala.)
Foreign Relations—J. W. Fulbright (D–Ark.)
Government Operations—John L. McClellan (D–Ark.)
Judiciary—James O. Eastland (D–Miss.)
Finance—Russell B. Long (D–La.)
Agriculture and Forestry—Allen J. Ellender (D–La.)

House Committee Chairmen

Rules—William M. Colmer (D–Miss.)
Ways and Means—Wilbur D. Mills (D–Ark.)
Interstate and Foreign Commerce—Harley O. Staggers (D–W.Va.)
Judiciary—Emanuel Celler (D–N.Y.)
Government Operations—William L. Dawson (D–Ill.)

House Committee Chairmen

Foreign Affairs—Thomas E. Morgan (D–Pa.)
Banking and Currency—Wright Patman (D–Tex.)
Armed Services—L. Mendel Rivers (D–S.C.)
Appropriations—George H. Mahon (D–Tex.)
Agriculture—W. R. Poage (D–Tex.)

Source: Thomas R. Dye and L. Harmon Zeigler, The Irony of Democracy *(Belmont, Calif.: The Wadsworth Publishing Co., Inc.), p. 249.*

[1] Deceased 1969; replaced by Hugh Scott.
[2] Replaced Dirksen as Minority Leader, 1969; replaced as Minority Whip by Robert P. Griffin (R–Mich.)

ment is, "Indeed the women do not participate equally with the men." [14]

When it comes to the *informal relationships* so crucial to the successful maneuvering and power play within Congress, indications are strong that women are, again, virtually excluded. What goes on in the men's clubs and bars, on golf courses, and in gyms can be of great significance in terms of exchange of information, nurturing of friendships, swapping of confidences and promises. The fact is that women are simply not invited to and not particularly welcome in these informal gatherings. Middle-class mores, male chauvinism, quaint chivalry—either or all characteristics contribute to their exclusion. How complete and how devastating this can be is indicated in the remarks of a male administrative aide to one of the congresswomen:

> No woman can ever make it. The power structure doesn't operate that way. So much of the power structure is built around the golf course, the bar, over cards, in the gym shower room, etc. I doubt that the best or most able of women can ever get into the inner circle where there is complete acceptance. There are always some differences. Particularly is this true among Southerners; she is not accepted there as an equal. Where the men may banter and tease about an

14. Geblen, "Women in Congress," p. 40.

issue—"Hey Joe, what do you mean by adding that amendment; trying to break the country?" sort of thing—with her they just say, "Why, certainly, Mrs. Blank, I'll think about it." But they don't. They give deference, but they don't give any real attention.[15]

Who else has power in the federal government? There is, of course, the president's Cabinet. Appointive offices all, here *might* be an arena where the recognition of women's needs and abilities is not inhibited too much by the possible prejudice of the greater public. The president, as the leader of all the people and the spokesman of the whole nation, could surely be expected to take cognizance of the fact that women now have full political membership in this country—and a potential majority of votes as well. One might expect that his appointments—to the Cabinet and to other high offices—reflect this reality, by now more than a half-century old.

But no. Since 1920, only two women have held Cabinet rank in the federal government. They were Frances Perkins, Secretary of Labor, 1933–45, and Oveta Culp Hobby, Secretary of Health, Education and Welfare, 1953–55. Neither the liberal President Kennedy, the reportedly prowoman President Johnson, nor the professedly fair-minded President Nixon found it opportune to select one member of the majority group of this nation to serve in their Cabinets.

Women do fare better in lower-level appointive offices, it is true —just a little better. In the foreign service, for example, all of 10 have served as ambassadors and ministers between 1920 and 1970. At the present time, we have 103 chiefs of mission abroad and only 3 of them are women. The Foreign Service has 3,061 women among a total of 10,769 employees. Among Foreign Service Officers, however, women constitute *less than one-tenth* of the total.[16]

But women are doing well in the Foreign Service in comparison with other branches of the federal government. Of the 849,421

15. Ibid., p. 39.

16. U.S. Civil Service Commission Statistics Section, *Study of Employment of Women in the Federal Government: 1967* (Washington, D.C.: Government Printing Office, June, 1968).

women in federal civilian service in 1968, only *147* held the top positions, grades GS 16 through 18. That makes for 1.5 percent of women among the administrators and federal executives who may be assumed to have significant influence and/or authority in the fields of policy-making and/or implementation.[17] Table 4.2 tells a by now familiar story.

Table 4.2

FULL-TIME WHITE-COLLAR EMPLOYMENT:
GENERAL SCHEDULE AND EQUIVALENT GRADES
(OCTOBER 31, 1968)

Grade groups	*Total employment*	*No. of women*	*% of women in grade group*	*% of total women employed*
1–6	1,113,059	525,381	47.2	78.7
7–12	672,753	132,865	19.7	19.9
13 & above	171,594	6,409	3.7	1.0
16 & above	(9,635)	(147)	(1.5)	(0.02)
Ungraded*	6,464	2,579	39.9	0.4
Total	1,963,870	667,234	34.0	100.0

Source: U.S. Civil Service Commission, Manpower Statistics, Study of Employment of Women in the Federal Government, 1968 (*June, 1969*), *p. 4.*

* For the most part, "ungraded" are support staff to the federal judges and courts throughout the U.S.

It is important to note, too, that in several of the agencies centrally located in the policy-making apparatus there are *no* women in the top positions (rank 16 and above). Neither the National Security Council, the Office of the Secretary of Defense and Joint Chiefs of Staff, nor the Atomic Energy Commission has women in rank 16 or above. The Bureau of the Budget and the Council of Economic Advisers each have *one* woman in rank 16, and *none* above.

In the judicial branch of the federal government, *no* women are to be found in positions above the rank of 12, and in the Department of Justice, only 5 made it into rank 16 and 1 into rank 17.

17. *The 1969 Handbook on Women Workers,* p. 121.

By comparison, 338 men in that department enjoyed ranks of 16 and above in 1968.[18]

There is, of course, no need to elaborate on the absence of women on the Supreme Court. Not only has no woman been *selected* to serve in that crucially important office, but none of the fair sex, the majority of citizens, have been seriously *considered* for such an appointment. There were, on the other hand, five women among the District Court Justices in 1968, one in the Court of Customs, two in the Tax Court, and three serving in District of Columbia courts by presidential appointment.

The dismal record of women's share of decision-making positions in the legislative arena is not even matched, then, by their share of power in the executive and judicial branches of the federal government. The virtual absence of women in top positions in these areas, positions that carry with them the responsibilities, the access, and the prestige that guarantee influence and/or authority, provides overwhelming evidence of women's lack of representation in the nation's political power structure. Vote or no vote, as far as formal power in the federal government is concerned, women just have not made any breakthrough yet.

III.

Can the picture be improved upon by looking at the legislative and executive positions within state and local governments? Or are women once more to be found outside the main arena where influence is brought to bear, decisions made, and public policies implemented?

Again, the scene is quite easily surveyed. And again, women are notable for their absence and not their presence.

The most important office on the state level is, generally speaking, the governorship. The record shows that only three women

18. U.S. Civil Service Commission Statistics Section, *Study of Employment of Women in the Federal Government,* p. 4.

have succeeded in being elected governor since women got the chance to run for and elect candidates to this exclusive position. All three of them, moreover, owe their success to something other than recognition of their own personal assets and/or the right and fairness of electing a member of the majority to this office. Each of them succeeded husbands who had held the post before them, and in the case of two out of the three, it was widely recognized that they ran in lieu of their husbands, who promised to and did run the administration for them.

In the case of Miriam A. ("Ma") Ferguson of Texas, her husband, a former governor, had been impeached and was therefore disqualified from running for office. "Ma" Ferguson, whose husband had disapproved of the women's rights movement, was in office from 1924–26 and again from 1932–36. Her campaign slogan was "Two governors for the price of one." [19] Lurleen Wallace of Alabama was the other woman to stand in for a husband frustrated in his desire to run for the governorship. It was only when Governor George Wallace failed in his attempt to change the state constitution to permit his re-election in 1966 that he put up his wife as the nominal candidate for the office he wanted for himself. The campaign made it very clear that a vote for her would be a vote for him. It made for an easy victory. Lurleen Wallace's short and dependent career ended with her death before her first term in office was over.

The third woman governor in the history of these United States, Nellie Taylor Ross of Wyoming, did not even do any campaigning when she was elected in 1925 to fill the unexpired term of her husband. Being in mourning and having no political experience, she left all of that to her male campaign manager.[20] Her victory, one may assume, had more to do with sympathy and nostalgia than with any rational or ethical factor.

Among the other important executive offices in state government, offices to which accrue a significant amount of independent power and prestige, we find the advances of women to be not quite, but very nearly, as few and far between. Only one woman has served

19. Ibid., p. 22–94.
20. Gruberg, *Women in Politics*, pp. 189–90.

as Attorney General and only three as Assistant Attorney General. Three women have served as Lieutenant Governor.

The positions women have been accepted in are either those where the women workers outnumber those of men or those where administrative experience counts for more than political pull and women have had a chance to acquire the former. In all, 38 women have served as superintendents of public instruction. As we know, the vast majority of teachers are women. It must be emphasized that *most* of the state superintendents are still male. The other fields in which women have made greater inroads are either outside the policy-making arena or quite remote from political power. Women apparently are gaining acceptance in the jobs of Secretary of State, Treasurer, and Auditor. In 1967, seven each were elected Secretary of State and Treasurer.[21]

Another centrally located institution in the power structure on the state level is the State Supreme Court. We find only 3 women sitting on this bench in 1968. We may add that among the nation's judges generally, 8,748 in number in the same year, there were only 300 women.[22] That comes to less than a 3 percent representation for women in a governmental branch invested with formidable power, the kind of power that directly affects the lives and fates of millions of citizens yearly.

In the domestic policy-making area, it is of course the state *legislatures* that continue to dominate. Representation in these bodies is important for anyone with a stake in decisions affecting education, law enforcement, crime prevention, welfare, health, housing, and a number of other areas of public concern.[23] In the domestic area 62.1 percent of all public expenditures were handled by state and local governments in 1966 and in the preceding five years the percentage had been slightly higher. The noise and clamor of lobbies

21. *The 1969 Handbook on Women Workers,* p. 125.
22. Gruberg, *Women in Politics,* p. 190.
23. The importance of state and local government in these areas is indicated by the public expenditures of the federal and state governments. In 1966, for example, the federal government spent $58.025 million on domestic programs. State and local government spent $94.906 million. U.S. Bureau of the Census, *Statistical Abstract of the United States: 1967* (Washington, D.C., 1967).

and interest groups in every state legislature in the nation is a telling indication of the importance attached to the decision-making power of the incumbents.

The issues dealt with by state legislatures are also of the type that women are presumed to have a greater interest in. The success of women in breaking into this portion of the man's world is therefore of special significance. How well do they do?

The answer is, and it is almost becoming repetitious at this point, very badly indeed. In 1967 women held only 318 out of 7,700 state legislative seats. That adds up to about a 4 percent representation of women in state legislatures, generally. In the upper houses of the legislatures, invested with greater power and longevity in office, women held only 45 seats. There were, in fact, 20 states in which women had *no* representation in the upper house. This was true, for instance, in two of the most progressive states of the union, New York and California. To complete the picture, it should be added that in New York women had 5 out of 150 seats in the House of Representatives and in California they had 3 out of 80 in the lower chamber.[24]

Looking at the power structure within the state legislatures, the impression of an all-male world is further confirmed. No more than five women have acted as floor leaders for their party, and only two as speakers of the statehouse. A mere three women have acted as presidents pro tem of the upper houses.[25] The lack of advancement of women into these formal positions of leadership is of special importance, since it is through these offices that the much-disputed committee assignments are handled. Viewed in the light of the great weight given to informal relationships, another area in which women are greatly handicapped, the absence of women on this top level takes on added significance.

24. *The 1969 Handbook on Women Workers,* p. 125.
25. Gruberg, *Women in Politics,* pp. 179–81.

IV.

Is it any better, then, in the government that is "close to home"—the local units?

For once, the answer is yes—although the affirmative is a heavily qualified one. Although only 100 women were serving as mayors in 1966, there were reportedly thousands of women in county and city posts. New York State's Governor's Committee on the Education and Employment of Women reported in 1964 that there had been a 37 percent increase of women officials and administrators in the preceding decade.[26] It must be emphasized, however, that this hardly amounts to a breakthrough. We have to look at not just the number, but at *what kinds* of positions are held by women and how much political power is entailed in each. The reasons for women's greater activity and success on the level of local politics are also revealing of the real status and access of women in the political life of this nation.

For one thing, there is not a single woman mayor of a major city in the United States. In the city councils and on boards of supervisors in metropolitan areas, women have, in fact, achieved no more representation than they have in Congress or in state legislatures. It is as library board members, treasurers, treasury clerks, and finance commissioners that women have found their way into governmental councils. Moreover, their limited success in this area is to be attributed largely to two factors: one, local positions are frequently part-time and poorly paid—there are comparatively few men who can and will seek them; and two, given the relatively nonpartisan character of these local offices, they are considered more "suitable" for ladies than the highly competed for and power-invested posts on other levels of government.

One important elective position more open to women and—one must conclude—of special interest to them as mothers and as teachers, is that of school board member. This is an important post because it is through the school boards that the school budget is dis-

26. Ibid., p. 201.

persed, educational standards set, curricula and teachers approved. The potential for power here is obvious—such decisions have a direct bearing on shaping the minds of the young, influencing not just their careers, but their very life styles. Strikingly, women amount to no more than 9.7 percent of the school board members in the nation, according to the National School Board Association. More than half of the boards reported they had no women members at all. Of the remaining half, only 12 had more than one woman sitting as a member. Here, it appears that only in the big cities have women gained acceptance in a field of policy-making they would seem eminently suited to. Women constitute 23 percent of big-city school boards.[27]

And so the picture is complete. In terms of formal political power, in terms of their proportionate share of representation on the decision-making levels in federal, state, and local government, women are left out or take a back seat even more systematically and dramatically than in the socioeconomic realm. The presumed "power" of the American woman turns out to be a myth— if anything, a greater myth than the stereotyped belief that the American woman is secure, pampered, and spoiled in this best of all worlds—for females.

V.

One question comes immediately to mind in reviewing the dismal record of women's share of political power. Is it because women are less active in politics that they do so poorly for themselves?

First, let us look at women's choices at the polls. There has always been and still is some difference in the voting activity of men and women and every major election will turn up speculations about and jocular references to the "women's vote" by party pros and observers of the scene. Women are supposed to be more candidate-oriented than men, more easily impressed by the apparent virility and good looks of male candidates, and less rational, that is, interest-

27. Ibid., p. 215.

oriented in their choices, than are men. The evidence for these assertions is by and large unimpressive—unexamined assumptions and
tired old clichés seem to be of the essence in most. As to the male sex
appeal supposedly influencing women voters, Clare Williams, a
former director of the Women's Division of the National Republican Committee, has the following retort: "If Marilyn Monroe was
running against Eleanor Roosevelt, I suppose some men would
be influenced, too." She adds, "I don't feel that Bob Taft was a
handsome man, yet women rallied behind him fervently." [28]

Her Democratic counterpart, Katie Louchheim, is equally firm in
rejecting the theory: "If there is any secret to reveal about dealing
with women it is that . . . they cannot be won over by virile
masculine smiles, honeyed compliments, and precious prose. In
1944, Wendell Wilkie was a fine figure of a man, but look what the
Republicans did—they threw him out for the little man on the
wedding cake." [29] And the wedding-cake man, one might add, went
down to defeat in a contest with crusty old Harry Truman, at that
time hardly distinguished either by sex appeal or by the "fatherly
image" said to attract women to Dwight D. Eisenhower.

What serious research findings we have point to slight, but potent,
differences and will be discussed in the context of socialization processes and male and female roles in our society. Any review of policy
outcome, however, makes it clear that *if* there is a women's vote, it
certainly has not been put to use on behalf of women. As for partisan
preference, of female voters, these do not, as Professor Warren Miller concludes, differ markedly from those of men.[30]

Neither, it turns out, are there any significant differences between
the voting ratios of men and women. In fact, the differences have
been gradually reduced in recent years to the point where in the
1968 election, the turnout of women of voting age was 64 percent
and of men 67.8 percent.[31] A very slight gap, indeed. Certainly, it is

28. Quoted in Sidney Shalett, "Is There a Women's Vote?" *Saturday Evening
Post*, September 17, 1960, p. 80.
29. Ibid.
30. Quoted in Shalett, "Is There a Women's Vote?" p. 81.
31. U.S. Bureau of the Census, *Statistical Abstracts of the United States:
1969* (Washington, D.C., 1969), Table 536, p. 371.

as nothing compared to the veritable gulf in representation between the two sexes in the political arena.

Since women vote in very nearly as great numbers as men, then, can their lack of representation in governmental councils be explained by their abstinence from party politics and campaign activities? No, not as far as effort is concerned. The mere suggestion of such a cause is laughable to anyone remotely familiar with political campaigns and the role of volunteers in them. Were it not for the willing and hard-working women throwing themselves into the "nitty gritty" of campaign activities and maintenance of volunteer organizations, it is a fair bet that the present party structures would quickly come to a point of collapse. Very few candidates would be so rash and foolish as the Republican congressman who cavalierly dismissed women willing to work their fingers to the bone for his re-election: "Well, girls, don't get too upset about it," he is reported to have told them. "My organization is running smoothly, so don't you worry your pretty little heads." The "girls" didn't, according to Clare Williams, and the congressman went down to defeat against a candidate with a less patronizing attitude towards women.[32] It is worth noting that it was not just the general preference by women for the Eisenhower candidacy that made his victory into a landslide, but the fact that about 6 million women volunteers were reported to have worked eagerly in his campaign.[33]

Reluctant and strangely fearful recognition was given to women party workers by a prominent male activist some years ago. Wrote John Fischer, editor of *Harper's* magazine: "Note who actually does the political work in your own community. Who is it that sells tickets to the Annual Dinner, mails out reminders to register, gives tea parties for the Peerless Leaders, keeps minutes at committee meetings, drives voters to the polls on election day? Nine times out of ten a woman. The insidious fact is that they work harder." [34]

What is *insidious* about it, according to John Fischer, is that one day they might just take over. He waxes positively lyrical in conjur-

32. Shalett, "Is There a Women's Vote?" p. 80.

33. Ibid.

34. Quoted in Marian V. Sanders, *The Lady and the Vote* (Boston: Houghton Mifflin Co., 1956), p. 31.

ing up this abhorrent spectacle: "One of these mornings all of the district leaders in the country will stroll down to their club rooms, chomping their cigars without a worry in the world. When they open their doors they will find the windows have been swathed in pastel curtains, the spittoons and pinochle decks thrown out, the poker layouts converted into vanity tables, and all those cracked and cherished leather chairs draped in chintz. And if they don't like it, the ladies will be ready and able to elect a bunch of Ardent Amateurs to take their place. It's later than you think."

It turned out that John Fischer and other male defenders of the fort had little to fear, after all. As of 1970, women were no closer to the reins of power in politics than they were in the mid-fifties. But the attitude towards women in politics revealed by this prominent liberal intellectual is by no means atypical. Women in politics still tend to be typed as "fluttery females—or bespectacled battleaxes," as Katie Louchheim protested in 1960.[35]

The prevailing pattern in party politics is now, as then, to encourage "the girls" to come out and work in campaigns and to generally rely on them for volunteer clerical services, but to give them a cold and even hostile shoulder if they have ambitions beyond that. This is the norm, according to a number of women who made it against the odds.[36] India Edwards, for many years the vice-chairman of the Democratic National Committee, reports: "If the party backs a woman you can be pretty sure they do it because they think it is a lost cause but they know they have to have *some* candidate." Her observation is cheerfully affirmed by John Bailey, former chairman of the Democratic National Party: "The only time to run a woman is when things look so bad that your only chance is to do something dramatic."[37] And Clare Williams tells of a certain county chair-

35. Quoted in Shalett, "Is There a Women's Vote?" p. 80.
36. Sen. Margaret Chase Smith, Rep. Margaret Heckler, Marian Sanders, Kate Louchheim, and Clare Williams are but some of the women politicos who have talked of the resistance of party big-wigs to their career plans. Three of the eight prominent women discussed in Peggy Lawson's *Few Are Chosen* (Boston: Houghton Mifflin Co., 1968; p. xxiii) had to run for office without party endorsement.
37. Ibid.

man's reluctant sanction of the first woman candidate of his party to run for Congress in his district. His admonition to a group of women volunteers was: "Ladies, I've never approved of women on the ticket and this is the first time I've permitted a woman to become a candidate. I want to tell you that if you don't turn out as big a vote for her as for a man, there'll never be another woman on the ticket." [38]

As late as mid-1970, the quaint and yet deep-rooted prejudices not uncommon to political king-makers were given quite spectacular voicing by none other than a liberal member of the Democratic Party's Committee on National Priorities. His remarks came in response to a request by Democratic Congresswoman Patsy Mink of Hawaii for her party to "give the cause of women's rights the highest priority it deserves." Dr. Edgar F. Berman, a close personal friend of former Vice President Hubert Humphrey, turned a cold shoulder to her appeal, claiming that women were subject to raging hormonal differences which disqualified them for high public office. Said Dr. Berman: "Suppose we had a President in the White House, a menopausal woman President who had to make the decision of the Bay of Pigs. All things being equal, I would still have had a male JFK make the Cuban missile crisis decisions than a female of similar age who could possibly be subject to the curious mental aberrations of that age group." [39]

Dr. Berman's flat disclaimer of women's ability to govern was, naturally, not allowed to stand unchallenged in a period of feminist ferment. Rep. Patsy Mink, in a widely publicized letter, urged Hubert Humphrey to seek Dr. Berman's resignation. "I am certain you will be appalled," she said, "at Dr. Berman's disgusting performance in which he displayed the basest kind of prejudice against women, characterizing us as mentally incapable to govern, let alone aspire to equality, because we are physiologically inferior." The aftermath to this interesting contretemps was to offer further revelations of the status of women in American politics. Hubert Humphrey's response to Patsy Mink's challenge to get the "medieval" Dr.

38. Quoted in Shalett, "Is There a Women's Vote?" p. 80.
39. *San Francisco Chronicle*, July 31, 1970, p. 17.

Berman to resign, was simply to tell her it was a matter between the two. One can well imagine what would have been the outrage on the part of this most liberal champion of causes had it been a different minority so blatantly maligned by a close political associate.

Incredibly, Dr. Berman himself denied harboring any prejudice against women, pointing to his support of liberal policies in the past. Only after NOW and prominent feminists got into the fray and public exposure of Dr. Berman's views threatened to embarrass the party was he asked to resign by male co-members of the Democratic National Committee.[40]

To sum up, neither the turnout at the polls nor the involvement and effort in party activities by American women can be blamed for their conspicuous lack of representation in elective offices at all levels of government. Clearly, it is prejudice that stands in their way, prejudice among male power-wielders in the parties, for one thing, and possibly also inhibitions and self-denigration among women political activists themselves. The latter is a problem of formidable dimensions and profound implications for the quality of political life, and can best be explored in the context of political socialization. It is ultimately the lack of political consciousness and group cohesion among most members of this vast "under" class which must be changed if women are to gain the opportunities and advantages sought by the feminists. Yet the important point to be made here is that women's input into the political process entitles them even now to a far greater share of the decision-making positions in the system and to a much greater portion of the politically allocated goods and benefits of the society as well.

Women representatives of the Ninety-First Congress have offered telling testimonies of the difficulties they encountered in running for office. "Even when a woman demonstrates a strong base of support," says Margaret Heckler (Rep.–Mass.), "usually the party hierarchy is the last to see your potential as a candidate." [41] Patsy Mink points to the shortage of campaign funds for women candidates. It is, she

40. Ibid.
41. This and the remarks of the following four women are cited from the *Congressional Quarterly*, Weekly Reports, July 10, 1970, p. 1746.

says, "partially the result of not being taken seriously by politicians." Although they will go all out to raise funds for the campaign of a rising young man, "they will not do this for a woman." Rep. Catherine May (Rep.–Wash.) points out that the new accent on youthful vitality begun in the Kennedy years also puts women at a disadvantage. Family responsibilities usually keep women from entering politics until late in life.

One of the strongest statements came from Shirley Chisholm, black congresswoman from New York: "When I decided to run for Congress, I knew I would encounter both antiblack and antifeminist sentiments. What surprised me was the much greater virulence of the sex discrimination. . . . I was constantly bombarded by both men and women that I should return to teaching, a woman's vocation, and leave politics to men."

Rep. Julia Butler Hansen (Dem.–Wash.) finally put the problem in its proper social context: "Every essence of a woman's life prevents her involvement in politics." Quite simply, "the problem is related to the larger question of a woman's role in society."

And so it would seem. We shall take up that question after examining the presumed power of women in other spheres of America's social life.

Five

POWER'S OTHER FACES

One of the characteristics of myths is that they don't die easily. They persist, in fact, against evidence and in contradiction to the rules of logic and are cherished not for their rational content, but for the comforting or alluring explanations of reality that they offer.

So it is with the myth of woman's power in our society. It is clung to by a great many with little or no basis in reality to support it and it is so hotly defended as to suggest an elaborate system of defense mechanisms in operation. The overbearing woman and the downtrodden male are fantasy figures dear to the hearts of many Americans, as witnessed by the incessant use of these themes in the communication media. Whether these figures are treated in a comic vein or seriously attacked, no cognizance is taken of actual power relations in American society. The male comes out the victim, whether as the dear, trusting clod of a henpecked husband or as the viciously manipulated and "castrated" son of the symbolic Jewish mother. And woman, shame be to her, incessantly conspires to take over, to get or keep the reins of power in her mysteriously strong little hands. Charming she may be while she is at it, but devious, always devious; vile, even, in the vituperative attacks of a Philip Wylie, an Edward Albee, or a Philip Roth. Lacking other devices to interest the public in her "powers," television writers and producers will go to such lengths as to cast her in the role of a witch or genie— in a modern-day setting, yet. The great popularity of the television programs "Bewitched" and "I Dream of Jeanie" in recent years may offer testimony if not to outright superstitions, at least to the persistent preference among a section of the American public for the myth of woman's supernatural powers. After all—how many *male* witches or genies have we seen on TV lately?

Like all other social phenomena, myths serve certain functions. To discover what these are we have to have a very clear view of the social reality portrayed by a myth and then extrapolate what interests and needs are served by its maintenance. Our examination of both the job market and the political arena indicates very strongly that the particular myth of the power of women in America turns reality on its very head. We must admit, however, that there are other faces of power to be examined. In a pluralist democracy like America, authoritative power, that is, the enforceable right to command others, resides primarily in governmental institutions; but influence, that is, the ability to manipulate the social situation of others or their perception of it, is a special type of power that is distributed in a more complex and elusive manner.[1]

It is, of course, institutionalized power that we are interested in. The power or influence one person may have over another in an intimate relationship is not a very fruitful subject for social analysis. Let it merely be said here that if there were any truth to the supposition that in such situations it is women who are in command or women who can manipulate the actions or perceptions of men, it would stand to reason that this advantage would be used to gain for women benefits and opportunities in other social situations. The whole sorry history of the suppression of women—in all realms of life, up to and including our time—makes a mockery out of the vulgar theory of woman's "bedroom power." The influence a woman may have in a relationship of intimacy with a man may be used to ameliorate her personal situation, but *not* to change her social one.

In examining institutional power we must, moreover, make a distinction between power of position and power of property. The former belongs to the incumbent of any social role or organizational

1. The definitions offered here are from Gerhard E. Lenski, *Power and Privilege* (New York: McGraw-Hill Book Co., 1966), p. 7.

office endowed with rightful authority or influence. It is a temporary power, in the sense that persons in possession of it will lose it when they vacate the positions to which it attains. The power incumbent upon owners of great wealth or property does not depend upon incumbency in any office or role—it can be and often is dissociated from it. Wealth and property can, however, be put to use in a variety of ways for the purpose of manipulating the social situation of others or their perception thereof. To mention but a few: Contributions to political campaigns can make or break candidates or force certain issues upon the attention of the public and make for ignoble neglect of other topics, thereby affecting policy outcomes that may have a profound impact upon the daily existence of most of us. Controlling ownership of business properties can be used in such a manner that it changes the very quality of life in a community; decisions of where to locate and when to vacate affect not only the livelihood of people, but also traffic patterns, pollution, and the tax base of the locality. Wealth can also be parlayed into formidable power when channeled into advertising and full or partial control of the media. The influence these institutions have on our perceptions of social reality is obviously very strong indeed. Wealth can also be used to set up or support tax-exempt foundations or endowments to universities, thereby influencing the direction and use of research in the academic community.

The question of where power resides in America is as complex as it is controversial, but there should be no need, in this instance, to re-open that particular hornet's nest.[2] It is clear from the foregoing analysis that we see the possession of wealth and property as a *power resource* rather than as actual power. What we are trying to do in this part of our study is to identify which institutions in American society exercise control or dominant influence over social situations and the way we perceive them, and then to find what is

2. Interested readers are referred to: Robert Dahl, *Who Governs* (New Haven, Conn.: Yale University Press, 1961); Peter Bachrach and Morton S. Baratz, "The Two Faces of Power," *The American Political Science Review*, LVI (1962), 947–52; C. Wright Mills, *The Power Elite* (New York: Oxford University Press, 1959); and G. William Domhoff, *Who Rules America?* (Englewood Cliffs, N.J.: Prentice-Hall, Inc., 1967).

the role or place of women on the decision-making level of these institutions. We are not concerned, therefore, with the "idle rich," but with *the governing elites*, the persons directly involved with and to varying degrees responsible for the operation of the corporate economy, the shaping of the American polity, and the formation of the educational process.

The central importance of governmental institutions to the whole network of social relationships has already been pointed out. Our examination of women's share of power in this area showed that it was practically nil; the representation of women on all levels of government is disastrously short of even the most flexible notions of what is fair and proper and cannot, therefore, be interpreted as anything but a power vacuum in regard to women. What remains to be seen is whether the absence of women on decision-making levels in politics is repeated in other centers of power in our national life. Where, if anywhere, is the much-reputed power of women to be found?

I.

We shall start with the corporate economy. Here we are greatly aided in our task by finding general acceptance for the hypothesis that effective control is in the hands of a relatively small number of very large corporations, banks, and insurance companies. As G. William Domhoff points out, there are "awesome statistics buttressing this statement." The nature of control in these large businesses does not present us with much of a problem either, thanks to the summation and impressive analysis presented by Domhoff in his *Who Rules America?* Most authorities, he affirms, find control in the hands of the boards of directors, a relatively small group of individuals who meet regularly to decide upon major company policies. Minor decisions and technical research can be delegated, it is true, but investment policies, for example, and the selection of management are decided by the board. Stockholders do not, by and large, interfere and extremely few of them have the kind of holdings that might make for any influence in these situations.[3] In 1953, Robert Lampman found that 1 percent of the population held 28.5 percent of the wealth in the United States, and within that 1 percent, a much smaller percentage had the bulk of these holdings.[4] Analyzing these and other figures offered by prominent economists, Domhoff reaches a conclusion similar to that drawn by C. Wright Mills in *The Power Elite*: ". . . At the very most, 0.2 or 0.3 percent of the adult population own the bulk, the pay-off shares, of the corporate world." [5] More often than not it is such substantial shareholdings that give access to corporate directorships.

In his examination of this corporate elite, Domhoff suggests that one can learn enough about this group by focusing in on the top 20 industrials, the top 15 banks, and the top 15 insurance companies. What he sought to examine was the social class of the incumbents, while we are interested in their sex. His method makes sense, however, and—like him—we can make a very long story short by pointing out that all of the 884 individuals in question were men. Not one woman was among them.[6] Some minor improvement has, however, taken place recently. Our separate study of the top 15 insurance companies in 1969 found all of 8 women among the 201 men on their boards of directors.[7]

Looking at *all* large banks and corporations, Dr. Margaret Cussler confirms that only a handful of women are on the boards of directors of these institutions.[8] In 1956, *Fortune* magazine estimated that of the about 250,000 "real" executives in the country, a mere

3. Domhoff, *Who Rules America?* p. 38.

4. Roger Lampman, *The Share of Top Wealth Holders in National Wealth, 1956* (Princeton, N.J.: Princeton University Press, 1962), p. 202.

5. Quoted in Domhoff, *Who Rules America?* p. 45.

6. Domhoff, *Who Rules America?*, p. 51.

7. The fifteen companies and information about their directors are taken from "Moody's Insurance and Financial Stocks—Monthly Reference List," December 8, 1969.

8. Margaret Cussler, *The Woman Executive* (New York: Harcourt Brace & World, Inc., 1958).

5,000—2 percent—were women.[9] It is a fair bet that these are still in the middle management positions, rather than on the highest levels. As late as 1969 women in retailing, the most traditional female executive stronghold, occupied but an "infinitesimal" number of first-rank executive positions, according to William Burston of the National Retail Merchants Association.[10] The same year found 270 women among 14,172 bank chairmen or presidents, but it is indicated that the majority of this lucky 2 percent presided over small family banks and owed their positions to inheritance.[11] A *Business Week* survey of women in business at this time (1969) found that American industry produced as few top women executives as it had ten years earlier.[12]

Whether one chooses to emphasize directors or high-level executives as the important power-wielders in the corporate economy, it is clear that women are just not cut in. To be really thorough, we might also examine how many women are to be found among corporation lawyers, since these are known to be closely linked to the business elite and to have an influence that "goes far beyond the giving of advice on legal matters." [13] Both C. Wright Mills and A. A. Berle, analysts of widely different political views, point to the central role played by the corporation lawyer. Mills finds him performing the function of the "go-between" effectively and powerfully; transcending "the narrow world of any one industry," he is "in a position to speak and act for the corporate world or at least sizeable portions of it. The corporation lawyer," concludes Mills, "is a key link between the economic and military and political areas." [14] Berle affirms that the law firms "become virtually an annex to some groups of financial promoters, manipulators, or industrialists." Not only do they dominate the legal profession, "what they have contributed . . . is the creation of a legal frame-

9. This figure is equivalent to approximately 2 percent of the total number of "real" executives in this country at that time.
10. *Business Week*, August 2, 1969, p. 44.
11. Ibid.
12. Ibid., p. 42.
13. Robert A. Gordon, quoted in Domhoff, *Who Rules America?*, p. 59.
14. Mills, *The Power Elite*, p. 289.

work for the new economic system, built largely around the modern corporation." [15]

We gain a very good insight into women's role in the power-invested world of corporate law from an authoritative study by Erwin O. Smiegel.[16] First, it should be pointed out that the influential law firms are usually very large and that most of them are situated in New York or have branches in that city. Of the 1,755 women attorneys in New York, Erwin found only 18 listing themselves as working in large offices. In the New York city branches of the large firms with headquarters elsewhere, only one woman law partner could be found. Women, it turned out, were usually not even given a chance to enter corporation law. Of the lawyers who wished to engage a law clerk, considered to be the springboard to a career in this field, 90 percent refused to even interview women lawyers for the job. Interviews of the few female associates found revealed that they felt they had little chance to advance to partnership. Large law firms, they pointed out, were too much like male clubs—women were simply not wanted.

II.

The absence of women among the governing elite in the corporate economy is the more conspicuous for the fact that women do account for about *one-third* of the top wealth-holders in this country.[17] Also, in recent years women have accounted for slightly more than 51 percent of the adult shareholding population. The number of shares owned individually by women stockholders equaled 18 percent of the total as compared with 24 percent owned individually by men. The remaining 58 percent were held by institutions, brokers and dealers, persons with joint accounts, nominees, and

15. A. A. Berle, Jr.. *Encyclopedia of the Social Sciences,* IX (New York: The Macmillan Co., 1948), p. 341.

16. Erwin O. Smiegel, *The Wall Street Lawyer* (New York: The Free Press, 1964).

17. Lampman, *The Share of Top Wealth Holders,* p. 100.

foreign owners.[18] Although these figures already belie the assertion that women own most of the wealth in the country, their share of it certainly seems to be large enough for at least the small minority of wealthy women to gain access to decision-making positions in the corporate economy. So what has happened here?

Apart from the customary prejudices and inhibitions operating in this as in all other institutional settings, it must be pointed out that women's control over their share of wealth in America is subject to a number of qualifications. First, they come into it at an older age than do men. More than one-third of the women wealth-holders examined by Lampman are widows over 60 years of age and most of them inherited their holdings from a deceased husband. Of the remaining women among the top wealth-holders, about three-quarters are married and they are usually the beneficiaries of bequests and transfers set up by their husbands or fathers to take advantage of loopholes in tax legislation.[19] More than twice as many women as men, affirms Sylvia Porter, obtain their first share of stock through inheritance or as a gift.[20] Also, more women than men are the beneficiaries of estates left in trust.

The implications of these findings are quite clear: Women wealth-holders are not likely to have the expertise, the experience, or the opportunity for putting their resources to use in an attempt to influence the trend and shape of the economy. This conclusion is affirmed by several of the top financiers of the country. Veteran Wall Streeter Gerald M. Loeb points out that stock ownership by women does not mean that they handle their own financial business. "As a matter of fact," he says, "I rarely see a woman handling her own account—it's usually a banker, a broker, her attorney, or a relative, *but it's a man.*"[21] Albert E. Schwabacher, Jr., a San Francisco investment banker, also discounts the theory that women are about to take over the economy. They may own about half of

18. *The 1969 Handbook on Women Workers*, pp. 145–46.
19. Sylvia Porter, "Did Women Cause Panic Black Monday?" *Sacramento Bee,* June 18, 1962, p. 11.
20. Ibid.
21. Lampman, *The Share of Top Wealth Holders*, p. 241.

the *personal* property in the United States and perhaps a smaller percentage of the real estate, but much of it is handled by professional managers and brokers. "My own guess is," says Schwabacher, "that they actually control not more than 15 to 20 percent of our total national wealth. Obviously, this constitutes neither a national emergency nor a national opportunity." [22] A vice-president of Merrill Lynch, Pierce, Fenner & Smith affirms that women are not nearly as important in trading as people think—only one out of every five of their stock customers is a woman. In 1962, for example, women accounted for only 25.5 percent of all trading on the New York Stock Exchange.[23] At the same time, it must be remembered that only a tiny minority *within* the minority of women stockholders have the amount of shares necessary to make their influence felt in the management and operations of major corporations.[24] That, together with the other factors limiting women's effective use of their wealth holdings, makes all of the noise and furor about women's take-over of the economy nothing but ludicrous.

III.

There is one more institution to consider as we examine the exercise of power in the corporate economy. Organized labor has, in the past few decades, established itself fairly securely as a group with influence and something close to a veto, if not affirmative decision-making power, in the economic and political system. The governing elites in the corporate system are clearly somewhat restricted in their exercise of control by the activities of labor, on the levels both of bargaining and of political action. As an interest group, labor constitutes one of the most formidable

22. The Sacramento *Union*, November 22, 1955, p. 9.
23. Sylvia Porter, "Did Women Cause Panic?," p. 11.
24. Robert Lampman reports 253,000 women with gross estates of $60,000 or more in 1953. Lampman, *The Share of Top Wealth Holders,* p. 191.

elements in what Schattschneider has called "the pressure system":[25] the conglomerate of interest groups and private associations that are supposed to serve as the link between the individual citizen and the government. *How much* weight can be assigned to labor in the operation of the pressure system is still a matter of controversy; but even though "the flaw in the pluralist's heaven," in Schattschneider's caustic words, "is that the angels sing with an upperclass accent," [26] labor must be conceded the ability to halt or to restrain, if not always to block, corporate acts not to their liking.

Women do have a place in the labor movement, as we know. With nearly 38 percent of the work force being women, they very well should. Although they are not to be found in unions with the ratio we would expect given their participation in the labor market, there were still 3,689,000 women union members in 1966. One out of every seven women workers belongs to a union, compared to one out of every four men workers. Also, 88 percent of women members belonged to the AFL-CIO and the remaining 12 percent to unaffiliated unions.[27] Among union members in 1966, one out of every five was a woman.

We should expect, therefore, that at least in this sector of our social life women have gained a significant share of decision-making power and a chance to influence the shape and direction of the corporate economy. Like most other organizations, however, the AFL-CIO is effectively controlled by an oligarchy of leaders. The executive council of the AFL-CIO is most important in the hierarchy, but local leadership also exerts authority over union members, as well as representing them in negotiations with employers. Union hierarchies have, in a sense, "edged into the process of industrial administration," according to V. O. Key, "and have a hand, through bargaining, in the formulation of policy on promotions, transfers, layoffs, fringe benefits, methods of production, and other such matters. If we regard the process of governing as the impo-

25. E. E. Schattschneider, *The Semi-Sovereign People* (New York: Holt, Rinehart and Winston, 1969).

26. Ibid.

27. Data from *The 1969 Handbook on Women Workers*, pp. 82–83.

sition of rules of behavior, unions in reality govern as well as agitate." [28]

For us the question becomes, then: Have women made it into the union hierarchies? And an examination of the *Directory of National and International Labor Unions in the United States, 1967,* provides us with the data we need to ascertain women's power in this area. There is, first of all, the Executive Council of the AFL-CIO, with 28 members in all. *No* women are listed here. On the Council's standing committees, 16 in number, *no* woman has been appointed chairman. On the staff of the Committee, we find *one* solitary woman. She is the librarian—hardly a position endowed with power.[29]

In the listings of the officers of national and international unions, we do, however, come upon an occasional representative of the fair sex. In the 191 organizations, 128 of which are in the AFL-CIO and each of which has several officers, we find all of 31 women officers. Astoundingly, even in 2 large unions where at least *80 percent* of the membership is female, the leadership turns out to be *all male.* Thus neither in the Amalgamated Clothing Workers of America nor in the International Ladies Garment Workers' Union, is there one woman officer on the national level.

This sample should suffice as a conclusive indication that women in the labor movement are as devoid of power in their special sphere as are women in political and economic life in general. Not only are they cheated out of the share of representation in the hierarchy that their membership ratio entitles them to; they have virtually *no* representation at all.

In 1962, labor leaders organized a conference in Washington on the problems of working women. Man after man came to the podium addressing the women assembled—"in fawning tones"—as leaders.[30] It was too much for one "peppery grandmother of 65,"

28. V. O. Key, Jr., *Politics, Parties and Pressure Groups,* 4th ed. (New York: Thomas Y. Crowell Co., 1961), p. 65.

29. U.S. Department of Labor, Bureau of Labor Statistics, Bulletin No. 1596.

30. Barbara Bates Gunderson, "The Implication of Rivalry," in Seymour M. Farber and Roger H. L. Wilson, eds., *The Potential of Woman* (New York: McGraw-Hill Book Co., 1963), pp. 165–85.

Bessie Hillman, who took to the microphone to express her annoyance. Men in the movement, she contended, deliberately ignored women—not one woman was on the 31-member executive council of the AFL-CIO and not one woman had ever been sent abroad to represent the big labor federation at international conferences. The 150 women assembled were *not* leaders: "Not one of you is on the executive or policy-making level of the union," she pointed out. "They let you be shop stewards, business agents, education directors." [31] Woman after woman at the conference had declared that their greatest problem was sex discrimination, but Mrs. Hillman put the problem back in the lap of the organization itself. Union leaders, she contended, "are the worst offenders as far as discrimination against women is concerned." [32]

To sum up, the U.S. corporate economy is run, managed, and/or controlled with very little aid or hindrance from the women of the country. Women have little or no representation among either the governing business elites or the hierarchy in labor unions that have a chance to direct and shape this enormous economic enterprise. That women are important as consumers is obvious enough, but the "countervailing power" [33] of the consumer can hardly be said to be more than a fond memory or a distant hope in this age of high-pressure advertising, oligopolies, and price fixing. Given the present impotence of women as a pressure group in the political arena,[34] the power void confronting women in this additional important sphere of our national life is very serious indeed.

31. Ibid., p. 184.
32. Ibid.
33. The term is used by J. K. Galbraith.
34. Women are represented in the "pressure system" by two groups: The League of Women Voters, a civic study group with 106,000 members (1960), and NOW (National Organization of Women), with about 6,000 members. Only NOW maintains a lobby strictly by and for women.

IV.

Power in the mass media is power to be reckoned with in modern society, for the messages transmitted through newspapers, radio, television, and magazines have considerable influence on our perception of social reality in general and on our political orientations in particular. We no longer have a society of publics, where there is frequent interaction between people on the intellectual and political levels and where people formulate different viewpoints on the basis of this interaction, organize around them, and compete for their viewpoint to win out in the arena of politics. In a mass society, as C. Wright Mills points out (and we have moved a considerable distance towards it), the dominant type of communication is the formal media; publics become mere markets for these media. The ebb and flow of discussion must still be considered and informal opinion leaders can be important in changing perceptions and attitudes; but then, *their* messages, too, are by and large transmitted through the media.[35]

This is not to suggest that we are confronted with an all-powerful, monolithic force set to brainwash and manipulate the American people. The media convey to us different images, conflicting messages, and varying interpretations that afford and encourage clashes of opinions among individuals and, on the whole, scholars in the field have found effective mass communication to function more frequently as an agent of reinforcement than as an agent of change.[36] Yet the media are crucial in carrying through political messages today. Access to and effective use of television, for instance, can build up candidates and focus attention upon issues that would

35. For an examination of the role of opinion leaders in the context of a media-dominated society, see: Elihu Katz, "The Two-Step Flow of Communications: An Up-to-Date Report on an Hypothesis," *Public Opinion Quarterly*, XXI (1957), 61–78; and C. Wright Mills, "Mass Media and Public Opinion," in I. L. Horowitz, ed., *Power, Politics and People: The Collected Essays of C. Wright Mills* (New York: Ballantine Books, 1963), pp. 577–99.

36. These findings are effectively summarized in Richard E. Dawson and Kenneth Prewitt, *Political Socialization* (Boston: Little, Brown and Co., 1969).

otherwise be destined to obscurity. The meteoric rise in politics
of Governor Ronald Reagan of California, for example, and the
against-all-odds success of Cesar Chavez' drive to organize farm
workers, could not conceivably have come about without television's spotlights. Reagan, before 1966, was a likable, but not
too prominent, actor whose political aspirations occasioned surprise or chuckles among most Californians; then he captivated TV
audiences with his highly polished deliveries of messages dear to
their hearts. And Chavez was a missionary without money, influence, or the power of a large following; then the plight of farm
workers and his fight on their behalf was dramatized by TV,
bringing liberal and radical sympathizers flocking to his cause.
Power to affect the political orientations of people is perhaps the
most crucial form of power in a democracy; as already suggested,
it is only through politics that institutional arrangements and resource distribution can be effectively and seriously challenged.

How do women stand, then, in regard to this important resource
in American society? What is their representation among decision-
makers in the media, that is, among the groups and individuals
with authority to fire and hire communicators, to accept and re-
ject programs and messages, and to initiate new approaches and
test them in the field? Also, how do women figure among the communicators themselves? What inroads have they made in the areas
of writing, interpreting, editing, and producing for any and all of
the media? Here should be a very important measure of the *influence* of women on the perceptions held of themselves by both
sexes. Here is also to be found a good measure of their part in
shaping the American polity, as G. William Domhoff terms it.

The major networks must be attended to first. On the board of
ABC, there was not one woman among the 15 directors in 1970.
At NBC, one woman director found her way in among 17 male
colleagues. And at CBS, there was one woman among 15 males.
In surveying presidents, vice-presidents, and general managers of
television stations throughout the country, we find *no* women in
this influential group in all of 37 states. In the remaining states,
California had 4 women in 34 such positions, Georgia had 1 in 13,

New York 3 in 33, New Mexico 1 in 7, Ohio 1 in 28, Pennsylvania 3 in 26, Texas 2 in 51, Idaho 1 in 7, Illinois 1 in 23, Kansas 2 in 8, Kentucky 1 in 8, Nebraska 1 in 11, South Dakota 1 in 10.[37]

Having confirmed that women are quite some way from obtaining dominance among decision-makers in this vital media, we can move on to ascertain their influence among the creators and opinion-wielders in this field. The same *International Television Almanac* that provided us with the above data reveals that among those listed in the "Who's Who" of the grand "wasteland," there are only 10 women producers, 3 producer-director-writers, 2 commentators, 40 writers, and 20 executives. Not much of a showing either, for the female half of the nation.

In the major newspapers and magazines of the country, women have hardly made a dent into the field of editing. They are, for that matter, conspicuously absent as major political and cultural commentators as well. We do, however, find a few female interlopers on the boards of some major newspapers. The Washington *Post,* Houston *Post,* Chattanooga *Times* and New York *Post* each have one woman on their governing boards. The last newspaper mentioned is outstanding in that its lone woman on the board is not only the publisher, but also the editor-in-chief; Dorothy Schiff is also the majority stockholder in the New York *Post.*

V.

America's universities, debunked in common parlance as the "knowledge factories," have a special relationship to power. By themselves, these institutions do not have the capability to challenge and effect change in present power arrangements; yet by educating scholars and intellectuals they may have a decisive influence on what knowledge is to be transmitted and how it is to be used. Thereby, power structures will be affected, either in the direc-

37. Charles S. Aaronson, ed., *International Television Almanac* (New York: Zwigley Publications, 1969).

tion of reinforcement or in the direction of rejection. Ideas can be formidable weapons. The intellectual's superior ability to either justify or debunk authority makes him politically relevant—a source of potential trouble as well as necessary sustenance for the governing elites of a democracy, for in our society power has to be legitimized or, at the very least, concealed. Its possessors have to have earned their positions, according to our most basic beliefs. The consent of the governed must be obtained—or their indifference to the arrangement insured. And it is when these subtle and yet explosive political questions come up that intellectuals figure prominently on the scene. The main reason for the mounting attacks on universities in the late sixties may very well be the increasing and well-publicized unwillingness on the part of their incumbents to accept and cooperate with the status quo. The massive research coming out of the top universities must be kept flowing to its places of destination, be it corporations, agri-business, or government. In the status quo perspective, students and their professors must be kept in line to the point, at least, where they do not interfere with that flow or succeed in arousing significant portions of the public to challenge present power structures.

As both faculties and students have sadly come to realize, it is the boards of trustees or boards of regents of the universities that have the real power in this sphere. Faculties, no matter how well organized, have found themselves undercut and overlooked on so many occasions that it is clear that their "autonomy" is subject to the tolerance and will of other power-wielders. College presidents hold some sway still and can, with superior tactical skill, go a long way in making the boards accept policies and proposals considered essential by faculty and students. But college presidents, too, can be replaced—even summarily dismissed, as witness the recent case of one of the most superior tacticians among them, President Clark Kerr of the University of California. So it is to the boards we must look for the kind of power that can shape and direct higher education and its uses in America. And it is to the elite universities and the largest state universities we must look to find the institutions that influence and set the standards for the whole educational apparatus. Again, one must keep in mind the central importance of government to these operations—not just the state universities, but also the private ones depend on governmental subsidies and/or research grants today. But we already know the answer to our question about government; what we are after now is the share of power accorded women in the governing of higher education. And that, at this point, means primarily women's share of positions on the boards of trustees of the top universities. To a lesser, but significant extent, it also means women's representation on the boards of foundations giving substantial grants to universities.

We shall start with the boards of trustees.[38] In our examination of 21 major U.S. universities in 1969, we found that in 5 there were no women on the boards of trustees. The Universities of Kansas, Illinois, and Colorado, plus Yale and Harvard Universities, had not one woman representative among the 45 trustees on their respective governing boards. In the remaining 16 universities, there were 34 women among 492 men. That amounts to less than a 7 percent representation for the 51 percent majority of this country in this additional important sphere of America's institutional life. The universities examined were, in addition to the five mentioned above: the Universities of Georgia, Southern California, California, Iowa, Maryland, Minnesota, Wisconsin, Virginia, New York, and Pittsburgh, and Reed, Stanford, Duke, and George Washington Universities. Needless to say, none of these universities has a woman president.

The publicly supported system of higher education in California, considered a model for other states in most respects, offers an instructive example of the place and status accorded women in the governance of such enterprises. In the more than 100 years since the creation of the University of California (its "birthdate" is 1867), only 3 women have sat on its board of regents. One, no

38. Our data are derived from examination of 1969 college catalogues of the respective universities.

longer present, succeeded her husband upon his death. In the state college system, not one woman sits on the board of trustees. And on the level of junior colleges, only 42 women have made their way into the board, among 444 men.

The picture is hardly improved as we look at the governing elites among our major private or corporate foundations. Their total assets, tax free, were found to be $10.3 billion in 1963. The influence of the foundations is felt everywhere, as G. William Domhoff points out.[39] Their large grants go regularly to the arts, science, medicine, educational TV, and, most importantly, the university. This kind of funding naturally carries with it influence, if not commanding control over programs, teachers, and the direction and use of research. In the educational sphere, the names of the Ford, Carnegie, Rockefeller, and Danforth Foundations carry a very special weight. These are the sources for a great many of the programs, scholarships, and research grants without which the universities would be a great deal poorer both in breadth and depth offerings. Other foundations are of importance as well, but for our purposes, it should be sufficient to look at the sex composition on the boards of these four major ones. It is highly unlikely, after all, that the picture would change to any significant extent as we went down the scale.

The result is just as could be expected in view of our previous findings. On the Ford Foundation's board of trustees: no women. The Rockefeller Foundation: none. The Carnegie Corporation: one. And the Danforth Foundation: two.

In other associations or committees considered important in shaping the cultural-intellectual climate of this country, women are equally noted for their absence on the governing level. It takes but the briefest of looks to note the nearly exclusive male dominance in the five groups considered by G. William Domhoff in his analysis: The Council on Foreign Relations, the Foreign Policy Association, the Committee for Economic Development, and the National Advertising Council. If we are to pay attention also to the extensive and partially covert public relations programs of the CIA, the FBI,

39. Domhoff, *Who Rules America?*, p. 64.

and the various branches of our military, it is equally obvious that, again, women have little or no say.

We started this examination by suggesting that to discover the function of a myth we have to explore the social reality portrayed by it, for myths serve to conceal, to soften, and to rationalize our actual social relationships—to make them more bearable, as it were, both for those on the outs and for those favored in any common situation. Particularly when the reality is rather hard to bear, when the power relationships conflict with cherished principles of justice and fairness, when the victimization of fellow humans is too obvious and crude, myths are fostered and take hold among people. One might say, then, that myths serve us all well—except that as they obscure reality, they get in the way of needed change.

The myth of woman's power in America does just that. It does, indeed, turn reality on its very head and thereby it serves to imprison both men and women in a fuzzy, alluring fantasy that tends to immobilize anyone who wants to change the present power relationships. As long as the myth persists, as long as we continue to be blinded, women will have no more of their share of power than they do now. In the centers of power in our national life, what that amounts to is virtually *nothing*.

Six

THE IDEOLOGY OF SEXISM

Are women persons? The question was raised, tongue in cheek, by Adrienne Koch at a symposium on "Man and Civilization" arranged by the University of California a few years ago. Considering the pervasive and serious discrimination against women in every important sphere of America's social and political life, such an inquiry, it seems to us, ought to be taken quite seriously. In a society where the dominant creed calls for freedom, justice, and equality of opportunity for all, the existence of grave inequities and systematic subordination of a major group in the population can only be rationalized on the basis of a common belief that members of this group are somehow different, somehow outside the norm set for full-fledged citizens, somehow not quite equal. A degree of inferiority must be assumed in regard to women for members of both sexes to accept so willingly and unquestioningly the relegation of the feminine majority to a secondary status and a subordinate rank in every strata they have found their way into. Male domination has to be considered *normal* and woman's inferior assignation *proper* for the sexist institutions to function as smoothly as they do.

Such was the problem with blacks in American society at the time that Gunnar Myrdal took up his investigation of *An American Dilemma*.[1] It was a problem, said Myrdal, in the hearts of white

1. Gunnar Myrdal, *An American Dilemma* (New York: Harper & Brothers, 1944).

106

Americans—having in theory committed themselves to the "American creed," with the postulates described above, they could live with the institution of racism only by assuming the inherent inferiority of black Americans or by determinedly ignoring the existence of this national shame. For this situation to change, it was first of all necessary for black citizens to force the problem upon the attention of the American public, to confront their white countrymen with demands to end this intolerable injustice, and to make it impossible to evade and ignore this festering sore within the body politic. Then, and only then, could the problem be properly attacked and the practices and structures of racism be eradicated from American life.

Again, the parallel with the problems of women is striking. One important question left unattended by Myrdal was, however, how the members of a group suppressed so gravely for so long were to overcome the feelings of inferiority and the habits of deference inculated in them throughout their lifetime, for one of the most debilitating effects of racial prejudice, as Kenneth Clark has shown, is that the victims come to believe in and even cherish their "inferiority." [2] The "Uncle Tom" mentality had to be changed before victims of racism could start on their move. No easy task, that, given the fact that the whole socialization process was geared to make blacks believe in and accept their inferior roles.

It can, as we now know, be done. But it is crucial to understand that suppression of women, like that of blacks, rests ultimately on what is believed about their innate nature and their proper and necessary role in society. This sets the context in which decisions are made for and against giving access to and allowing the advance of women in any one field of activity and in which behavior is judged as either appropriate or inappropriate. Just as important, women's self-concepts are to a very great extent dependent on the core of imputed and preferred feminine attributes prevailing in the society. Rationalizations for discrimination against women are provided by just this set of interrelated beliefs and values in regard to woman's

2. Quoted in M. Homer, "Woman's Will to Fail," *Psychology Today,* November, 1969, p. 36.

real nature and proper place. What I am talking about here is an ideology—the ideology, I will suggest, of sexism. Its beliefs and postulates are well integrated, it functions to direct and guide social and political activity, and it rests on assumptions that are not reliably tested, but that to some degree are accepted on faith.[3]

—I.

What are the components of this ideology? They are easily discovered, actually—familiar to all of us, accepted without question by many, and challenged by only a few. Its first tenets are that woman is different from man, in psychological as well as biological make-up, and that she consequently has a different role to play in the human environment. The "true" nature of woman has been depicted—ad nauseam—not just in mass media and popular literature, but also by a seemingly endless line of psychologists, sociologists, and anthropologists eager to add their voices to the choir of sexist conformity. The basic idea is that for women—although no longer for other human groups, oddly enough—*biology is destiny*. The mere facts that she bears children and has menstrual periods make her the prey to hormonal influences that shape her temperament and abilities in certain distinct ways. Woman is supposed to be more emotional than man, less able to apply logic to problems and situations, more conforming, and less aggressive, but also more devious and superior, naturally, in possession of that mysterious "feminine" quality, intuition.

In its most benevolent forms, sexist ideology becomes paternalistic in its protective approach and fawning tone. Take, for example, this description of feminine "nature" offered by a highly praised and well-read marriage counselor, G. O. Payetter:

3. This is the definition of an ideology offered, for example, by William E. Connolly, *Political Science and Ideology* (New York: Atherton Press, 1967). For a more thorough discussion of the concept, see Karl Mannheim, *Ideology and Utopia* (New York: Harcourt, Brace and World, Inc., 1936), pp. 55–109.

Feelings, moods and attitudes . . . rule a woman, not facts, reason nor logic.

By herself, woman is all mixed up, but superb as an auxiliary. . . .

A woman is inanimate or on the defensive until you create a feeling such as praise. Then she goes all out.

Never scold or explain when she is angry, remember she is feeling, not thinking. . . .

Stop bossing; just manipulate her in her feelings. . . . The acquisition of knowledge and responsibilities does not lessen woman's need for support, guidance, control. Quite the contrary.

Why ask women when they only need to be told? Why ask women when they hope to be taken? [4]

Feminine virtues are, indeed, extolled in the most extravagant manner by precisely those who insist that woman cannot, because of her nature, aspire to the status and heights of achievement in politics or intellectual or artistic work attained by a man. The charm of women, their gentleness, and their sensitivity to the sufferings of others are invariably held up as qualities special to their sex and, moreover, as qualities so attractive that they more than make up for women's lesser abilities in other areas. The possession of such virtues should presumably be gratifying enough to women to leave them satisfied with a secondary status. Witness, for instance, the self-defense of Dr. Edgar F. Berman of recent "hormonal-rage" fame. Having put Rep. Patsy Mink and other women politicians firmly in place by insisting that "there just are psychological and physical inhibitants that limit a woman's potential," he hastened to add: "The same glandular secretions producing the reactions which you say do not exist, endow most 'real women' with their most endearing and genteel charms." And although these splendid characteristics do not make possible any great accomplishment by women, they are "charms which help balance and restrain the aggressive male. . . ." [5]

The position goes back to Freud himself, of course, the origina-

4. G. O. Payetter, "How to Get and Hold a Woman," quoted in Paula Stern, "The Womanly Image—Character Assassination through the Ages," *Atlantic Monthly*, March, 1970, pp. 87–91.

5. *San Francisco Chronicle*, July 31, 1970, p. 17.

tor of extravagant speculations about women's "penis envy." The intellectual creator of the defeat-inducing feminine triad—masochism, narcissism, and passivity—also had chivalrous compliments to pay to "the most delightful thing this world can offer us—our ideal of womanhood." Nature, he suggests, "has determined woman's destiny through beauty, charm, and sweetness." [6] To this imposing father of psychology, his chosen partner for life was, naturally, "my sweet child" or "my precious little woman." [7]

The "nurturant" qualities of woman, cherished so highly by sexist psychologists in their more benevolent moods, are also enthusiastically supported by modern sociologists. The terms change, as we move into another discipline, but the assumptions of biologically based attributes and their ascription remain the same. The female, in Talcott Parsons' analysis, becomes "expressive" and the male "instrumental." [8] This is the leading sociologist of recent decades speaking, and the traits that go with these descriptions complement precisely those proclaimed to be feminine or masculine by psychologists, according to "Parsonian" Orville G. Brim.[9] For a woman to be expressive means, on the positive side, for her to be kind, obedient, cheerful, affectionate, and sensitive. All very well—until we compare these "proper" qualities for woman with their counterparts for the man and speculate on the political implications following from such assignations. For a man to be expressive means to be tenacious, curious, ambitious, responsible, original, and competitive—all qualities required of a governing class. The nonaggressive, highly emotional, submissive, cheerful, and affectionate member of the other sex—the "natural" woman as composed by psychology and sociology—is perfectly suited to take second place. Gunnar Myrdal's descrip-

6. Ernest Jones, *The Life and Work of Sigmund Freud*, I (New York: Basic Books, 1953), p. 175.
7. See Ernest Freud, *Letters of Sigmund Freud* (New York: Harcourt, Brace & World, Inc., 1960), p. 161.
8. Talcott Parsons and R. F. Bales, *Family, Socialization and Interaction Process* (New York: The Free Press, 1955).
9. Orville G. Brim, Jr., "Family Structure and Sex Role Learning by Children," in Robert Winch, Robert McGinnis, and Herbert Barringer, eds., *Selected Studies in Marriage and the Family* (New York: Holt, Rinehart and Winston, 1962), pp. 286–87.

tion of the situation of the black citizen[10] applies equally as well to that of woman: her assumed graces and her assumed vices fit her very appropriately for the inferior position assigned to her, for with the "nurturant" qualities and charms of woman go her masochism, envy, and narcissism, according to Freud—or her tattling, teasing, jealousy, exhibitionism, negativism, affinity for quarrel, and inability to cooperate, according to Brim.

We all know this "natural" woman. How deeply ingrained her image is in folk-culture is easily perceived by surveying popular literature, the media, and even children's books. In her analysis of popular magazines and movies in the post-World War II period, Betty Friedan found that almost without exception the "real" woman was depicted as submissive, nonambitious, and totally oriented towards loving and caring for man and children. The woman who escaped this norm, determined to go against her destiny in pursuing a career, was invariably described as frustrated, insecure, and masculinized, and, of course, was doomed to failure or perpetual gloom.[11] Such heart-warming images have also penetrated television, and with a vengeance. The typical woman here—in commercials, dramas, or situation comedies—is unpredictable, emotional, and irrational, but mixes her feminine wiliness with just the proper amount of feminine sweetness to, presumably, still appeal as a model of womanhood. Never, but never, is she a highly rational or ambitious figure with clear-cut career goals or dedication to something other than marriage, family, or courtship. If she, the poor thing, is found to be working in the man's world of business or professions, it is understood that this is a temporary affair, induced usually by widowhood—never, heaven forbid, by divorce. What she really wants is to stay at home and what she inevitably and perpetually is after is a man. In commercials, she is not only irrational and submissive—even to the strangest male intruders, often in ghost or sheik form—she is also helpless, so helpless that she will gladly follow the advice and direction of not only these weird samples of

10. Myrdal, *An American Dilemma.*
11. Betty Friedan, *The Feminine Mystique* (New York: Dell Publishing Co., 1963).

male superiority but also that of voices—male, naturally—coming out of walls. Susan Brownmiller, journalist and TV news reporter, said it: "The image of women in the commercials is that of *stupidity*." Actress Anselma Del-Olio adds that they picture woman as a "mindless boob or masochistic slave." And Ti-Grace Atkinson, writer and founder of the Feminists, points out what is obvious to many: "Women are shown exclusively as sex objects and reproducers —not as whole people." [12]

It is in children's literature that the put-down of women is started, however, and it is not hard to guess at its influence on the developing, accepting minds of young readers. Elisabeth Fisher, writer and editor, found "an almost incredible conspiracy of conditioning" as she investigated books for young children in stores and libraries.[13] There is, first of all, a serious omission. In the world of picture books, females appear in only about 20 to 30 percent of illustrations. Moreover, when girls appear, they are shown in their relation to boys and are depicted as passive, though sometimes manipulative. "They walk, read, or dream," Miss Fisher points out. "They seldom ride bicycles; if they do it, it is seated behind a boy as in Dr. Seuss's *One Fish, Two Fish, Red Fish, Blue Fish.* When I came across a little girl sailing paper boats, I was overwhelmed with gratefulness."

Working mothers don't exist in this never-never land of children's picture books. One book in which they do appear is known of, Eve Meriam's *Mommies Who Work,* but Miss Fisher found it out of stock in all the stores she visited. In other books the stereotypes of male activity, female passivity, male involvement with things and women's with emotions, and male dominance and female subordination persist. Comments Elisabeth Fisher: "Though there have been women doctors in this country for over a hundred years, and pediatrics is one of their preferred specialties, there is not a single woman doctor to be found. Women are nurses, librarians, teachers—but

12. Quoted in Edith Efron, "Is Television Making a Mockery of the American Woman?" *TV Guide,* August 8–14, 1970, p. 7.

13. Elisabeth Fisher, "The Second Sex, Junior Division," *New York Times Book Review,* May, 1969, pp. 6–44.

the principal is always male. They have emotions: they get angry; they disagree; they smile; they disapprove or are disapproved of; they want to please. What they do not do, is act. Boys do. Girls are —a highly artificial and unsatisfactory dichotomy."

The offense is repeated in school textbooks, from primary readers on. Marjorie Uren, of Stanford University, was shocked at the depth and pervasiveness of sex prejudice discovered in a great number of texts researched.[14] Women are either ignored—apparent noncontributors to history, civilization, and culture—or they are pictured in stereotyped roles as appendages or temptresses to men. Recently, the new line of textbooks adopted by the State of California for use in primary grades came under special scrutiny. Virginia Kidd, of the Department of Speech and Communication at Sacramento State College, found sexual roles dramatized in the following way:

> "Mark! Janet . . . !" said Mother.
> "What is going on here?"

> "She cannot skate," said Mark.
> "I can help her.
> I want to help her.
> Look at her, Mother.
> Just look at her.
> She is just like a girl.
> She gives up."

> Mother forces Janet to try again.

> "Now you see," said Mark.
> "Now you can skate.
> But just with me to help you." [15]

Janet, naturally, doesn't make suggestions of this kind to Mark. Mark's toys are the toys of adventure: a parachute, a rocket, a helmet, and so forth, and Mark aspires to be an astronaut. Janet's toys are all homebound: a playhouse, dolls, a buggy, dishes. But then,

14. Unpublished research, reported at a hearing of the California Legislature's Education Committee, May 12, 1970.
15. Virginia Kidd, "Now You See, Said Mark," *New York Review of Books,* September 3, 1970, pp. 35–37.

Mother's chief occupation in the readers is also washing dishes, cooking, ironing, sewing—and wearing aprons. Daddy's chief occupation is coming home—and playing ball with Mark.

Such are the images and such is the world that sexist ideology would proscribe for us. The inherent inferiority of the female of the species is subtly suggested and persistently conveyed in media-messages, textbooks, literature, and even science. We do not seem to have moved very far from the definition of femininity offered by Aristotle: "A certain lack of qualities; we should regard the female nature as afflicted with natural defectiveness." More than 2,000 years later, Vice President Agnew had this insight to offer: "Three things have been difficult to tame—the ocean, fools, and women. We may soon be able to tame the ocean; fools and women will take a little longer." [16]

II.

It is interesting to note that the psychologists' idea of woman's nature has provided sexist ideology with just the scientific cloak it needs in this age of egalitarian philosophies. On the basis of the "knowledge" that woman is less intellectually assertive, less ambitious, and more emotional than man, that she has less superego and therefore weaker social interests, one can with great ease assign her to traditional roles and to the place to which she was always accustomed—behind the man. The penis envy Freud considered to be a dominant theme in all feminine life, "inevitably causes women to feel inferior to men. These deep-seated feelings of inadequacy can be compensated for only partially by giving birth to a male child. . . ." Not just any child, mind, it has to be male. And "masochism and passivity . . . are natural aspects of normal femininity." From which follows, according to one of Freud's prominent interpreters, that "whenever a woman behaves in a nonpassive or ag-

16. Both statements are quoted in Stern, "The Womanly Image," pp. 88.

gressive way or competes with men, she is being neurotically unfeminine." [17]

What this all means in practical terms is spelled out with seeming satisfaction by other prominent psychologists. As late as 1965, Bruno Bettelheim of the University of Chicago could tell us that "we must start with the realization that as much as women want to be good scientists or engineers, they want first and foremost to be womanly companions of men and to be mothers." [18] For Erik Erikson of Harvard University, woman's mature fulfillment rests on the fact that her somatic design harbors an "inner space" destined to bear the offspring of chosen men, and with it, "a biological, psychological, and ethical commitment to take care of human infancy." [19] We will leave the final word with Joseph Rheingold, a psychiatrist at Harvard Medical School: "Woman is nurturance. . . . Anatomy decrees the life of a woman. . . . When women grow up without dread of their biological function and without subversion by feminist doctrine, and therefore enter upon motherhood with a sense of fulfillment and altruistic sentiment, we shall attain the goal of a good life and a secure world in which to live." [20]

Such conceptions provide new-found rationalizations, then, for sex-role standards and sex-role typing in our society. In our summary we shall rely heavily upon the succinct analysis offered by psychologist Jerome Kagan: These standards dictate to the female that she must feel needed and desired by a man and that her complete fulfillment in life can come only in raising and rearing a family. Dependency, passivity, and conformity is not only permitted, it is encouraged in the girl-child. For the male, on the other hand, sex-role standards stress the need to be independent in action, to dominate others, and to be able to control strong emotions, especially fear and helplessness. In America a boy is driven to prove that he is

17. Judd Marmor, clinical professor of psychiatry at UCLA, quoted in Stern, "The Womanly Image."

18. Quoted in Naomi Weisstein, *Kinder, Küche, Kirche as Scientific Law* (pamphlet) (Boston: New England Free Press, 1969), p. 1.

19. Ibid.

20. Ibid.

strong and powerful, and secondarily to arouse and gratify a love object. Other primary sex-typed behaviors are aggression—permitted in males, inhibited in females—and intellectual striving—encouraged in males, deprecated in females. A host of minor sex-typed attributes are transmitted in the growing process, and a person's sex role identity is developed according to how well his biological and psychological characteristics correspond to his or her concept of the ideal male or female. Ambiguity or frailty in this area is recognized as a source of severe stress and anxiety in many.[21]

How are these sex standards learned? Through the family, first of all, and through the education process, the media, the church, and, finally, peer groups. From infancy on, girls and boys receive messages contributing to their typing as either male or female, and usually, from the year two, some awareness of sex identity and sex standards has taken root. It is developed and reinforced at every step of the way from then on—as witness the images of mothers and fathers, boys and girls in the children's literature and textbooks discussed earlier. So subtle and pervasive are our preconceptions of sex attributes that we are most often not aware of how we channel boys and girls into distinct and different directions of development.

An instructive example of just such unconscious channeling is offered by teacher Julie Edwards of Davis, California. Comparing questionnaires submitted to parents of children in a private nursery school, Mrs. Edwards found that parents' approval and disapproval of qualities affecting their children's sociability could be clearly divided along sex lines. Parents of girls stressed their malleability, cooperativeness, and willingness to take direction as their daughters' most valuable characteristics. Disapproval was given to assertiveness and affinity to quarrel. Boys, on the other hand, were praised for being independent, assertive, and inquisitive, and severely put down for being timid and fearful.

The teachers' attitudes were found to correspond very well, indeed.

21. Jerome Kagan, "Check One: Male—Female," *Psychology Today,* July, 1969, pp. 39–42. See also Jerome Kagan, "Acquisition and Significance of Sex Typing and Sex Role Identity," in M. L. Hoffmann and L. W. Hoffmann, eds., *Review of Child Development Research,* I (New York: Russell Sage Foundation, 1964).

Watching the children play on the outside jungle gym, for instance, teachers would quickly interfere with a little girl having trouble in climbing up to the top: "Take it easy, dear—we'll help you down." But a boy trying the same daring feat would be cheered on: "That's the boy! You can make it if you want to!" Similarly, a girl acting aggressively would be put down for being bossy, while identical behavior in a boy would be dismissed with an easy-going shrug: "That's boys, you know." [22]

These conclusions have been confirmed in other research projects. In one wide-ranging study, *aggression* was found to be the area of behavior in which the greatest sex distinctions were made by parents. Preschool boys were allowed more aggression in their dealings with other children, while girls were rewarded for nonaggressiveness, conformity, and obedience.[23] W. A. Mischel agrees that from early childhood on, dependent behavior is less rewarded for males and physically aggressive behavior less rewarded for females in our culture.[24]

Few of us could claim never to have been guilty of such stereotyping in dealing with young boys and girls. Combined with the images projected in their reading material and transmitted through the media, the dictations of sex-role standards are bound to have a powerful impact on the personality development of members of either sex. This goes a long way towards explaining why and how it comes about that girls, for instance, tend to shy away from fields of activities considered adventuresome or intellectually taxing. It also provides clues as to how it comes about that as girls pass puberty, their drive to achieve in fields not recognized as "feminine" goes into drastic decline. Girls are, in fact, superior in academic achievement up to and through high school and they continue to do comparatively well in college. Yet fewer girl high achievers than boy

22. Unpublished research, reported at the Conference on Women, University of California at Davis, May, 1970.

23. R. R. Sears, Eleanor Maccoby, and H. Levin, *Patterns of Child Rearing* (Evanston, Ill.: Row, Peterson, 1957), p. 403.

24. W. A. Mischel, "A Social Learning View of Sex Differences in Behavior," in Eleanor Maccoby, ed., *The Development of Sex Differences* (Stanford, Calif.: Stanford University Press, 1966), p. 75.

high achievers go on to college and, while there, a very small proportion choose to major in fields like science, mathematics, economics,
medicine, and law. Even fewer go on to and complete graduate
school. The percentage of advanced degrees earned by women has,
in fact, been going down—from 13 percent in 1940 to 11.8 percent
in 1963.[25]

Psychologist Matina Horner has shown that, consciously or uncon-
sciously, girls equate intellectual achievement with a loss of femininity and that for girl students the desire to achieve is often
contaminated by the *motive to avoid success*.[26] This she defines as
"the fear that success in competitive achievement situations will
lead to negative consequences, such as unpopularity and loss of
femininity." [27] In a fascinating experiment, the standard TAT
achievement motivation measures were administered to a sample
of boy and girl undergraduates. Over 65 percent of the girls and
fewer than 10 percent of the boys showed evidence of the motive to
avoid success.

The full extent of sex typing upon the achievement and career
aspirations of women is shown dramatically in a study of college
graduates in 1961 conducted by the National Opinion Research
Center.[28] The women in the sample showed superior academic
performance throughout college and yet their career aspirations dif-
fered markedly from those of the men in the study. Among 33,782
college graduates, 11,00 women expected to pursue careers in elementary and secondary education, but only 285 hoped to enter
medicine, law, or engineering.

What must be understood is that the whole socialization process
is geared to discourage in girls any involvement and success in "masculine" pursuits, that is, pursuits that require ambition, daring, and

25. Robert M. Cunningham, Jr., "Some Women Who Made It Offer Insights
into Their Problems," *College and University Business,* February, 1970, p. 58.
26. Matina S. Horner, "Women's Will to Fail," *Psychology Today,* November,
1969, pp. 36–39, 62.
27. Ibid., p. 38.
28. James A. Davis and Norman Bradburn, "Great Aspirations: Career Plans of
America's June, 1961 College Graduates," *National Opinion Research Center
Report No. 82,* September, 1961.

inquisitiveness. Not only are such tendencies in girls the occasion for surprise and concern, so that they have to go against the advice and without the approval of most parents, teachers, or peers if they are to persist in their "masculinized" ways, but also, there are no female models for them to look to and follow—either in history books or in the educational texts generally. Nor for that matter are there more than a scattering of models in real life—women who have broken out of the imprisoning norms and accepted the challenges of an exciting, though often hostile, male-dominated profession.

There are additional burdens to carry for girls and women chafing under the strains imposed by sex standards. To seek and hold a man and to bear and raise his children is even more than just the ultimate fulfillment for a woman, our sex norms would have her believe. It is also her duty to her fellow humans and to society. To the charge of "penis envy" and "castration complex" that psychology has provided for use against women who choose to challenge male pre-rogatives, additional accusations of deviancy and destructiveness are levelled at these "masculinized" females from the anchor points of sociology and anthropology. The conventional wisdom of these disciplines would have us believe that the traditional division of roles between the sexes is "natural" and "good" for the society—even, some would add, "inevitable." The implicit assumption under-lying functional analysis in social science is that *persistence* in social arrangements is a test of validity, since every institutional phe-nomenon will be judged on the basis of its contributions to the stability or dynamic equilibrium of a society. Thus the ascription of sex role is considered fundamental to the maintenance and con-tinuance of any society and the particular sex standards and sex typing prevailing over time are therefore *functional*, that is, they contribute to the equilibrium of the society. A sociologist may pro-fess that this is not a value judgment, but the use of such terms as deviance, marginality, and pathology in the discussion of radical social innovations or of individuals breaking with traditional norms is not without persuasive implications. And naturally, in the context of sex-role development, such labels are applied to women and men who try to transcend the limitations imposed upon them by conventional sex typing. In the functionalist scheme of analysis, a challenge and attempt at change present a problem and not an opportunity. Adjustment and adaptation to present role structures is desirable and even essential. Rejection of present role structures and insistence on new ones imply a serious degree of pathology in the individual and a potentially destructive case of deviance for the society.

III.

As a consequence, the girl and boy growing up in America will receive messages throughout their education that reinforce the sex typing started in infancy. Even in universities, sex standards are not questioned—or were not until very recently. Female students are still primarily oriented towards finding a husband and raising a family—other interests and drives are discouraged and become illegitimate in society's view if and when they threaten to dominate. Society's expectations about the female role dictate to the female student that she be popular, desirable, marriageable, and able and willing to bear children. At the same time, society's dictations of what is desirable in a female preclude the development of independence of mind, intellectual inquisitiveness, assertiveness, and a drive to compete.

Such conditioning, we have to remember, is taking place at a time when egalitarian principles are uniformly recognized in institutions of higher learning and when the whole structure of public education rests on the acceptance of equality of opportunity, without regard to color, race, religion, or sex. The result is confusion, ambivalence, and emotional havoc among girls with talents or intellectual abilities. The result is also a damaged self-image and a decline in self-respect among the vast majority who cannot transcend the narrow stereotypes of behavior proscribed for them. How serious and widespread are these negative feelings among women is indicated by reports such as a *Fortune* magazine poll showing that more than one-fourth of women wish they had been born in the opposite sex[29] and a study of fourth-graders showing ten times as many girls wishing they could be boys as boys wishing they could be girls.[30] Women inevitably come to internalize the general disesteem in which they are held, as demonstrated by Philip Goldberg in his intriguing study: "Are Women Prejudiced against Other Women?" He found the answer to his question by testing the reaction of women undergraduates to an essay signed alternately by "John McKay" and "Joan McKay." The result, as expected, was that women downgraded the work of professionals of their own sex—not only in traditionally masculine fields, but in traditionally feminine fields as well.[31]

This confirms the fact that women view their differences from men as *deficiencies*, not just as complementary qualities offering equally valuable opportunities. Strikingly, this feeling is also typical among self-conscious minority groups. As Kurt Lewin has shown, group self-hatred is a frequent reaction of a minority group member to his group affiliation.[32] Personality distortion cannot be escaped, since a person's conception of himself is based on the defining gestures of others. Self-hatred is exhibited by a person's tendency to denigrate other members of the group, to separate himself from the average representatives of his group, or to be scornful of himself. Helen Hacker offers the following insight in her classic study, *Women as a Minority Group*:

> Certainly women have not been immune to the formulations of the female character throughout the ages. From those, to us, deluded creatures who confessed to witchcraft to modern sophisticates who

29. Quoted in Hacker, "Women as a Minority Group," *Social Forces*, no. 3 (1951), p. 62.
30. Godwin Wolson, "Psychological Aspects of Sex Roles," in G. B. Watson, ed., *Social Psychology, Issues and Insights* (Philadelphia: Lippincott, 1966, p. 477.
31. Philip Goldberg, "Are Women Prejudiced against Other Women?" *Transaction*, April, 1968, pp. 28–31.
32. Kurt Lewin, "Self-Hatred among Jews," quoted in Hacker, "Women as a Minority Group," p. 61.

speak disparagingly of the cattiness and disloyalty of women, women reveal the introjection of prevailing attitudes towards them. Like those minority groups whose self-castigation outdoes dominant group derision of them, women frequently exceed men in the violence of their vituperation of their sex.[33]

Even among women professionals, "the pattern of self-hatred and group disparagement is not untypical," as Cynthia Fuchs Epstein points out. Interviews with women lawyers found them frequently saying negative things about other women lawyers, suggesting that they, the others, suffered from personality disturbances, worked to compensate for their failures as mothers and wives, and the like. Nor did the interviewees care to be identified with "women lawyers" as a social category.[34]

Women's low evaluations of their own sex is also indicated by the finding that male babies are preferred over female babies by both parents.[35] Curiously, however, women who are apparently resigned to their traditional feminine roles usually protest their satisfaction with "being women." At the same time, *only 10 percent* of a large sample of housewives surveyed by Gallup would want their daughters to live the same way they have.[36] The remaining 90 percent would want their daughters to get more education and to marry later than they did. Also significant in this context is the disclosure of a 1968 survey that there are nearly 10 million housewives who would like to find some work to supplement their homemaking role.[37] One can only conclude that there is less fulfillment to be found in the traditional feminine assignments than our cultural king-makers and their loyal female following claim.

Some studies do, in fact, point to a very disturbing gap between

33. Hacker, "Women as a Minority Group."

34. Cynthia Fuchs Epstein, *Woman's Place* (Berkeley: University of California Press, 1970), pp. 26–27.

35. See, for example, Amitai Etzioni, "Sex Control, Science and Society," *Science,* CLXI (September 13, 1968), 1107–12.

36. George Gallup and Evan Hill, "The American Woman," *The Saturday Evening Post,* December 22, 1962.

37. Richard J. Schonberger, "Ten Million Housewives Want to Work," *Labor Law Journal,* XXI, no. 6 (June, 1970), 374–79.

reality and the sexist ideology's rosy portrayal of a fully feminine life. Dr. Alan Porter has found that wives are 60 times more likely to become depressed than single women. A three-year study of depression among his patients led him to conclude that "married women are prone to the disorder at any time in their lives and relapse is frequent." [38] These findings seem to be confirmed in an authoritative study of employed mothers in America, edited by F. Ivan Nye and Lois W. Hoffmann, which points out that working mothers are less likely than housewives to complain of pains and ailments in different parts of their body and of not feeling healthy enough to carry out things they would like to do. Employed mothers also show more self-acceptance and fewer physical symptoms of distress. They do, however, have doubts about their adequacy as parents.[39] But these, it would seem, result from social pressure rather than from any failure on the part of the working mother. No support was found for the view that working mothers have more difficulty with their children or are more negative in their feelings toward them than stay-at-home mothers.[40]

Another postulate of sexist ideology was disproved by a study on "Working Wives and Family Happiness" by sociologists Susan Orden and Norman Bradburn. In sexist folklore, it is the wife and mother who *wants* to work who is to be deplored. Her desire is suspect and indicative of a less than perfect adjustment to the proper nurturant role. For her to work because of economic need is, however, OK. Yet the two sociologists found that families of women who work because they *want to* are distinctly better off emotionally than families of women who work because they have to.[41]

But so powerful is the ideology of sexism, so ubiquitous and clamorous its doctrine, that despite all evidence to the contrary

38. A. M. W. Porter, "Depressive Illness in a General Practice: A Demographic Study and a Controlled Trial of Imipramine," *British Medical Journal*, no. 1, (1970), pp. 703–78.

39. Ivan F. Nye and Lois W. Hoffman, eds., *The Employed Mother in America* (Chicago: Rand McNally Co., 1963), p. 344.

40. Ibid., p. 330.

41. Quoted in Elizabeth Faneway, "Happiness and the Right to Choose," *Atlantic Monthly*, March, 1970, pp. 118–23.

women themselves have been emotionally entrapped in it. No greater tribute could be made to its persuasiveness than the continued insistence on the part of many women that all they want in life is wifely happiness and maternal fulfillment. The contrast in horizons and ambitions between women and men is here immediate and striking. What would we think, after all, of a man who professed such limited goals? For men it is human fulfillment that is to be sought—not just satisfaction in marriage and fatherhood. But, then, men are *persons*, individuals with needs and interests and drives that transcend their sex role. Women, it would seem, do not quite make it into that exalted category—or so sexist ideology would have it.

IV.

Our assertion that this body of beliefs, well integrated and designed to guide social activity, is a full-fledged ideology requires for its validity that we show it to rest on assumptions that are not reliably tested, but to some degree are accepted on faith. Well, then, what is known about the assumptions concerning woman's nature and her destiny in human society? Can they be said to be confirmed through the application of scientific method? Is there sufficient empirical data to support the far-reaching conclusions drawn by many psychologists, sociologists, and anthropologists?

We can start (as, in a sense, did the rest of these analysts) with Freud. The image of woman projected by the older Freudian school of psychoanalysis is that of a passive, masochistic, and narcissistic being. Freud's theory of woman's psychology was based on his observation of a universal feminine tendency, which he traced to early childhood experiences. This is "penis envy," which—according to Freud—inevitably takes possession of unsuspecting little girls as soon as they observe "the penis of a brother and playmate, strikingly visible and of large proportions." Naturally, to Freud, they "at once recognize it as the superior counterpart of their own small and inconspicuous organ . . . ," [42] and from this moment on a feeling of impotence will never leave the girl until her quest for the missing penis is sublimated in maternity. This presents fulfillment, then, "especially so if the baby is a little boy who brings the longed-for penis with him." [43]

The double blow dealt to woman here is quite a stunner, indeed. With such a handicap, it stands to reason that there is little use for her to aspire to equality with man. Every instance of dissatisfaction and rebellion can be put down to envy, to the desire to "castrate" a man. And then, as sublime maternity (a feat to be accomplished only with the cooperation of a man, mind) promises to relieve her of anxiety and frustration, it turns out that the product has to be male for ultimate fulfillment to be achieved.

Note, then, the "evidence" presented by Freud for confirmation of this most ambitious theory: He *observed*—and he *speculated*. There is, needless to say, no way to empirically test whether the phenomenon called "penis envy" has the universality and far-reaching implications claimed by Freud or, indeed, if it even exists. Girls lack the equipment in question, it is true, but then boys do not share in the complementary equipment of girls, either, and no theory has been put forth concerning an all-important "vagina envy" among the male sex. Indeed, to grown women the thought is rather ludicrous that a physiognomic part so vulnerable to damage, so unresponsive to command, and so awkwardly placed in terms of potential hurt and embarrassment should be something to want to have placed on one's own body.

The lack of such desire is indeed verified by the clinical experiences of psychiatrists like Clara Thompson[44] and Joseph B. Furst.[45] As Dr. Furst points out, the Freudian explanation is no explanation

42. Sigmund Freud, "Some Psychological Consequences of the Anatomical Distinctions between the Sexes," *Collected Papers*, V (New York: Basic Books, 159), p. 190.

43. Sigmund Freud, *Three Contributions to the Theory of Sex* (New York: Dutton, 1962), p. 127.

44. Clara Thompson, "Penis Envy," *Psychology*, VI, no. 2 (May, 1943).

45. Joseph B. Furst, *The Neurotic and His Inner and Outer World* (New York: The Citadel Press, 1954), p. 81.

at all. It is merely a huge argument in a circle, equivalent to saying that women have problems because they are not men.

It is the social context, we now know, that shapes and determines personality development. What a person does and who he believes himself to be will, as Naomi Weisstein points out, in general be "a function of what people around him expect him to be and what the overall situation in which he is acting implies he is." [46] Thus when women are found to be passive and narcissistic, such qualities should not be attributed, in the first place, to anything but the particular social conditioning women have been subject to and the social environment in which they continue to live. For these characteristics to be proved "basic" and inherent, we need more than mere theorizing about instinctual drives and bland assertions that biology is destiny. We need, for instance, documentation that these are the predominant characteristics of women in all known human societies over time and/or that women who do not possess them are not in possession of female physical characteristics and capabilities.

But such documentation has never been presented. On the contrary, what we have learned is that there are marked differences among cultures in the specific personality characteristics ascribed to women and men, as there are in the degree of differentiation between the two sex roles. In her now classic study, *Sex and Temperament in Three Primitive Societies,* Margaret Mead effectively demonstrated that in one society, the Mundugumor, both men and women tend to be ruthless, aggressive, severe, and unresponsive; in another, the Arapesh, both men and women had characteristics assumed in the West to be feminine—both sexes were unaggressive, cooperative, and responsive to the needs of others; and in the third society, the Tchambuli, the personality characteristics are the reverse of what we consider "natural"—women are dominant, impersonal, and managing and men are emotionally dependent and less responsible.[47] Historians as well as anthropologists have come up with evidence of matriarchal societies in the past, with indications

46. Weisstein, *Kinder, Küche, Kirche,* p. 3.
47. Margaret Mead, *Sex and Temperament in Three Primitive Societies.* (New York: Morrow, 1935).

that women exhibited anything but passive tendencies in their social relationships. Some sociologists, as well, have blasted the notion that there is a single set of characteristics defining women. In many places, it is pointed out, it is men who are thought to be emotional, sensitive, and intuitive, whereas women are thought to be cool and calculating. Modern Iran is a prominent example.[48] Scholars like Karen Horney, Erich Fromm, and Viola Klein have criticized the image of woman created by Freud and his followers. Says Viola Klein in *The Feminine Character*: "The realization that in different societies women fulfill different social functions, and accordingly display different attitudes and mental characteristics, has shattered the idea of the all-powerful influence of anatomy and biological traits on character traits." [49]

An example, now amusing, of the shallowness and fault in Freudian theorizing is the widely accepted notion, prominent in Freudian thought, that women have less sexual drive than men. Both this misconception and another Freudian maxim, that the vaginal orgasm is the only mature orgasm, have been exposed as bunk by the painstaking research in recent scholarship, in particular by Masters and Johnson in their massive study of the *Human Sexual Response*.[50] Women are, if anything, sexually superior to men in that they are capable of enjoying an infinite number of orgasms and are not dependent on the response of any one organ to enter into intercourse. Also, contrary to the idea that equality between the sexes would feminize men and masculinize women, thereby threatening satisfying sexual relationships, psychologist Abraham Maslow found after several studies that the more "dominant" the woman, the greater her enjoyment of sexuality, the greater her ability to give herself freely in love.[51] Alice S. Rossi summarizes his findings thus: "Women with dominance feelings were free to

48. Bernice C. Sachs, "Woman's Destiny—Choice or Chance," *Journal of the American Medical Women's Association*, XX, no. 8 (August, 1965), 733–38.

49. Quoted in Ibid., p. 733.

50. W. H. Masters and Virginia Johnson, *Human Sexual Response* (Boston: Little, Brown & Co., 1966).

51. A. H. Maslow, "Dominance, Personality and Social Behavior in Women," *Journal of Social Psychology*, no. 10 (1939), pp. 3–39.

be completely themselves, and this was crucial for their full expression in sex. They were not feminine in the traditional sense,
but enjoyed sexual fulfillment to a much greater degree than the
conventionally feminine women he studied." [52] This fact is cor-
roborated by Masters and Johnson. Yet to Freudians like Dr. Marie
Robinson, famed for her *Power of Sexual Surrender*, the driving,
competitive woman who is successful in the business world is "masculinized," and therefore *frigid*.[53] As to the immaturity of clitoral
orgasm, considered by Freud a sign of abortive emotional development in a woman, evidence is now in from many sources that there
is but one kind of orgasm, the clitoral. The Freudian distinction is
false to begin with.[54]

Need we explore further this maze of hazy theories and unfounded
assumptions to show that beliefs about woman's nature and destiny
are founded more on faith than on scientific evidence? More rigor-
ous dissections of this web of myths have recently been offered by
Naomi Weisstein, Anne Koedt, and Kate Millett.[55] Thus, in the
conclusion of psychologist Naomi Weisstein: "Psychology has nothing to say about what women are really like, what they need and
what they want, essentially, because psychology does not know." [56]
Jo Ann Gardner, president of the Association for Women Psychologists, essentially concurs: Psycho-therapists have reinforced the
standard sexual stereotypes of the society. They are therefore useless, or worse than useless, to women with emotional problems or
neurotic disturbances. Their concept of a mentally healthy female
is that of someone "passive, emotional, dependent, less competitive,
nonobjective, submissive, and more easily influenced—like the Ne-

52. Alice Rossi, "Inequality between the Sexes," in R. J. Lifton, ed., *The
Woman in America* (Boston: Houghton Mifflin Co., 1964), p. 139.
53. Quoted in Stern, "The Womanly Image," p. 177.
54. See, for example, Masters and Johnson, *Human Sexual Response*; and
Anne Koedt, *The Myth of the Vaginal Orgasm* (pamphlet) (Boston: New England Free Press, 1969).
55. See Weisstein, *Kinder, Küche, Kirche*; Koedt, *The Myth of the Vaginal Orgasm*; and Kate Millett, *Sexual Politics* (New York: Doubleday, 1970), pp. 157-235.
56. Weisstein, *Kinder, Küche, Kirche*, p. 3.

gro stereotype. . . . With the help of Freudian concepts, the thera-
pists are doing to women just what they are doing to blacks." [57]

The real and obvious differences between men and women—in
physical size, in muscular strength, and in physiognomy in general
—would appear to be of less and less consequence in terms of
abilities and achievement as technology and civilization continue
to advance. There are relatively few jobs left that require physical
strength and there are likely to be even fewer as years go by. And
whereas childbearing will remain an exclusive function of women and
childrearing may continue as a predominantly feminine vocation,
these tasks no longer consume more than a relatively small portion
of a woman's life. The evidence of testing now points to woman's intelligence and talents being no less than those of man's—the psychological differences observed are to a very great extent acquired
rather than innate. We do not, in the end, know what femininity
is, or indeed if there really exists such a cluster of traits and trends
that are not mainly derivatives of cultural forms.

Like all ideologies, the sexist ideology supports a structure that
leans more heavily on some groups than on others. It is, however,
too simple to conclude that women are the sole victims and to stop
short of further exploration into the costs of sexism. A system as
elaborate as this one and requiring for its support such ambitious
rationalizations is likely to damage more than the lives within its
"under" class.

We shall proceed to explore just what and who else are suffering.

57. Jo Ann E. Gardner and Charles W. Thomas (with George Harris), "Different Strokes for Different Folks," *Psychology Today*, p. 53.

Seven

DEMOCRACY AND OTHER VICTIMS

Social structure, socialization process, and ideology all interact to create a system in which women are deprived of their full humanity and shortchanged of their just share of social and economic benefits. This system, like all others, is ruled through politics; that is, it requires for its sustenance and perpetuation a political structure through which demands can be processed and from which commands can come forth and be implemented. The peculiarity in the situation of women in America is, as suggested earlier, that although they constitute a potential voting majority of this democracy, they have not come around to *using politics* to change the institutional forms of sexism and thereby improve their own life chances. By raising demands and by organizing to apply pressure on the political system, women have an excellent chance to change and end most forms of discrimination and oppression applying to them. In doing that they would, we will suggest, also change the very quality of American life and significantly upgrade the tone and character of our political dialogue. They might indeed make democracy a social and not just a political reality in America.

We should, by now, have a fair insight into the reasons for women's lack of efficacy in the political arena. The belief in women's innate inferiority and unsuitability for certain types of activities is the greatest obstacle facing those who would organize women. Male chauvinism may still create the greatest barriers, but women's acceptance of the rightness of their own inferior status makes them easy to control. As we have seen, "the entire society is geared to socialize women to believe in and adopt as immutable necessity their traditional and inferior role." [1] The values and postulates of sexist ideology appear to be quite effectively internalized in most women.

The question that must be raised at this point is this: *What does it do to a democracy*[2] to have half of its citizenry accept self-definitions that are bound to make their exercise of political rights and duties more difficult? Dependency, passivity, and conformity are all strongly endorsed and effectively cultivated feminine traits. How do they conform to the requirements of democratic citizenship? Is it possible that our stereotype of femininity and our ideal of womanhood come to constitute serious interference with a woman's positive orientation to and involvement with politics? Beyond that, what likely loss is endured by this nation as a consequence of the differential input into the system by half of its citizenry?

First, let us briefly examine what classical democratic theorists have had to say about the personal qualities called for in members of a democratic society. Although their conceptions of democracy do not always agree, they all join in the emphasis on popular participation in governing, either through elaborate systems of representation, as favored by James Madison, or by a direct and extensive involvement of all citizens, as suggested by Thomas Jefferson. The ideal is well stated by John Dewey: "The keynote of democracy as a way of life may be expressed as the necessity for the participation of every human being in the formation of values that regulate the living of men together." [3] Not only is the involve-

1. Marlene Dixon, *Why Women's Liberation?* (pamphlet) (San Francisco: Bay Area Radical Education Project, 1969), p. 4.
2. We shall come to grips with the problem of defining democracy later in this chapter. Meanwhile, we shall simply rely on the ideal conception of democracy as a system where individuals participate in the decisions that affect their lives.
3. John Dewey, "Democracy and Educational Administration," *School and Society,* April 3, 1937; quoted in Thomas R. Dye and L. Harmon Zeigler,

ment of citizens in political affairs necessary to ensure fair and acceptable policy outcomes, it is also desired for what it can contribute to individual self-development. Political activity, to these theorists, offers unrivalled opportunities for citizens to gain in knowledge and understanding and to acquire a sense of social responsibility. According to John Stuart Mill, the first question to ask concerning a particular form of government is: "What sort of human beings can be formed under such a regime? What development can either their thinking or active faculties attain under it?" [4]

Awareness, responsibility, and self-reliance are all considered essential qualities for the proper functioning of democracy and, at the same time, qualities desirable enough in themselves to choose the governmental form that would best foster them. The worth and dignity and creative capacity of each individual is assumed; it is this that makes possible a government of broad participation and maximum self-direction. The aim of government, on the other hand, is precisely the production of citizens responsible enough and capable enough to play this role. Neither Mill nor Jefferson believed that equality of talents and skills could ever come about, but they, like other democratic theorists, affirmed the moral worth of each individual and both the justice and necessity of everyone having a right to take part in the conflict over allocation of values in a society. Only broad participation could ensure that persons qualified for leadership would be found and selected and only active involvement in politics by all citizens would prevent undue power—the power that corrupts—from coming into the hands of a few. For Madison, it was not just the tyranny of minorities, but also that of a majority that posed a danger to human development. But for him too, the fostering of rationality, responsibility, and awareness in citizens was desirable, even if not always possible.

The contrast between these highly praised attributes and the characteristics of the conventionally "feminine" woman is as strik-

---

The Irony of Democracy (Belmont, Calif.: The Wadsworth Publishing Co., Inc., 1970), p. 6.

4. John Stuart Mill, *Representative Government*, quoted in Dye and Zeigler, *The Irony of Democracy*, p. 7.

ing as it is immediately apparent. Sweetness, passivity, and helplessness may be appealing qualities in a variety of situations, but
the political is *not* one of them. A woman whose self-concept is
entirely what sexist ideology would have it be is not likely to make
independent judgments, to voice her opinions, or to take on political responsibilities. Given the fact that intellectual inquisitiveness
is also ruled out as an attribute to femininity, she is likely to feel
discouraged from acquiring special knowledge of and consciousness about political issues. For her, a sophisticated and consistent
use of ideological concepts is apt to conflict with what she has been
taught are attractive personality features in a woman. A principled
vote, that is, a vote cast on the basis of political ideology, will
consequently not be her contribution to the democratic process.

To run for office—to compete against a man in an arena that
has for so long been a male preserve—must appear like a total im-
probability and an outrageous idea to the "feminine" woman. If
she still has a husband and children, this in itself is sufficient reason for her to abhor any role but her presently "proper" ones.
Even without them, her acceptance of what sexist ideology offers
as the image of ideal womanhood will very effectively prevent her
from taking on this particular responsibility of democratic citizens
—to seek, fight for, and accept the role of leader where occasions
call for it. Nor is she likely to be an "opinion leader" in her own
peer group; both her own self-concept and the reluctance of others
to accept political expertise in a woman get in the way of her exercising political influence in this manner.

It is not too much to say, then, that to the extent it has taken
hold, the effect of sexist ideology has been to disarm the American
woman politically and also to deprive American democracy of the
potentially informed and intelligent contributions of more than
half of its citizenry. From the point of view of classic democratic
theory, this is clearly disastrous. The model of citizen participation
and responsibility posed here cannot be approximated as long as
current sex standards and sex typing present serious obstacles to
women's entrance into the political arena.

Let us, then, examine the findings of voting experts and opinion researchers to ascertain whether our presumptions concerning the effect of sexist ideology can be affirmed. For the moment we shall leave aside the question, raised by the pluralist school in American political science, of whether the demands imposed by classic theorists on the citizens of a democracy are realistic and at all feasible. We need to know, first, whether there are discernible and significant differences in the way men and women in our society perceive politics and their own role within it. We need to know also how these perceptions influence the choices made by women at the polls and what difference, if any, this makes in likely policy outcomes over time.

I.

In 1937 an authority on political behavior concluded that "at every social level women vote less than men." [5] The difference in election turnout between the sexes has grown less significant as the years have passed, until in the national election of 1968 it was not more than 3.8 percent. In 1948 and 1954, however, there were still 10 percent more men than women exercising the right of franchise.[6] As stated earlier, the gap is by no means large enough to explain the near absence of women in elective offices on all levels of government, but it does suggest a lesser political involvement on the part of women generally. Apparently there is at least one group of women who experience a lesser social pressure to vote than men do. Interestingly enough, although women score just as high in approval of the system and attachment to the nation, their sense of *citizen duty* is at the same time somewhat lower than that of men. This leads Robert Lane, for one, to speculate that, for a good portion of the female nonvoters, it is the conventional views of

5. Herbert Tingsten, *Political Behavior Studies in Election Statistics* (London: P. S. King and Sons, 1937), p. 29.
6. Robert E. Lane, *Political Life* (Glencoe, Ill.: The Free Press, 1959), p. 210.

the proper female role that interfere with use of the franchise.[7] Such an impression is confirmed by the finding that we get the sharpest differentiation in voting turnout between men and women in the geographical areas and on the socioeconomic levels where sex typing is the most rigid.

In the South, in rural areas, and among people with only grade-school education, women make use of the ballot significantly less than they do in other localities and situations.[8] Lane quotes some of these nonvoters: ". . . Voting is for men." "I think men should do the voting and women stay at home and take care of their work." "A woman's place is in the home. Leave politics to the men." [9]

Although this particular cluster of phenomena—greater ratios of nonvoting among the least educated and poorest women in the population—may have a very serious effect on policy outcomes, the distinction between male and female political orientations can be more clearly shown by testing the sets of expectations developed by each sex towards the political system and their own role within it. This is where differences derived from sex typing are most likely to show up and where the deviance from the classic democratic models could be most serious. Effective political activity in a democracy requires both knowledge of issues, candidates, and processes and a certain competence in presenting one's views to political figures. A person's self-concept will have a great deal to do with his or her inclination and ability to acquire these necessary skills. We would expect women to generally rate lower than men in this area, given our cultural preference for nonintellectuality and passive compliance in females. Issue-oriented, politically sophisticated, and assertive citizens may be just what we need in this democracy—but as sexist ideology would proscribe, they had better not be women.

7. Ibid., pp. 210–12.
8. Angus Campbell, Philip E. Converse, Warren E. Miller, and Donald E. Stokes, *The American Vote* (Ann Arbor, Mich.: Survey Research Center, University of Michigan, 1960), pp. 486–92.
9. Lane, *Political Life*, p. 211.

And so it is, as we examine the studies now available on this very important problem. Sex typing and sex standards appear to affect political orientations from grade school on. The self-concepts of boys are clearly more appropriate for issue-orientation and active political involvement. Both girls and boys, for instance, list their father more often than their mother as the source of political information and advice.[10] And girls—it is generally accepted—learn their sex role by imitating their mothers. In voting literature, there are also recurrent reports of male political dominance in the family.[11] As could be expected, therefore, boys are both more interested in political stories and figures and better informed about them than are girls. The child's awareness of male political specialization is surely an important factor here—the nearly total absence of women models in history and government textbooks and in contemporary political life must be assumed to reinforce the girl's impression that "politics is not for women."

Among adults, the sharpest and most consistent differences between the sexes turns up in regard to the sense of political efficacy. Men are more likely to feel that they can cope with the complexities of politics and to believe that their participation carries some weight in the political process. The conclusion is clear, then, that although "moralistic values about citizen participation in democratic government have been bred in women as in men, what has been less adequately transmitted to the woman is a sense of some personal competence vis-à-vis the political world." [12]

Such a feeling of competence is, as noted earlier, an important prerequisite for effective political involvement in a democracy. But the greatest damage to democratic politics may yet come from the pervasive influence of sex-role definitions on the level of political sophistication among women. Table 7.1 tells the story. The ability to conceptualize, identify, and distinguish ideological abstractions,

10. Fred E. Greenstein, "Sex-Related Political Differences in Childhood," *Journal of Politics*, May, 1961, pp. 353–72.
11. Ibid., p. 364.
12. Campbell, *et al., The American Voter*, p. 491.

Table 7.1

RELATION OF SEX AND EDUCATION TO LEVEL
OF CONCEPTUALIZATION, 1956

	Grade School		High School		College	
	Male	*Female*	*Male*	*Female*	*Male*	*Female*
Level of conceptualization						
A. Ideology	8%	1%	17%	5%	34%	27%
B. Group benefit	43	33	52	44	36	34
C. Nature of times	30	26	19	26	19	21
D. No issue content	19	40	12	25	11	18
	100%	100%	100%	100%	100%	100%
Number of cases	251	291	354	537	175	155

Source: Angus Campbell, Philip E. Converse, Warren E. Miller, and Donald E. Stokes,
The American Voter, *Ann Arbor, Mich.: Survey Research Center, University of Michigan,*
1960), p. 492. Reprinted by permission of the Survey Research Center.

or at the very least group interests, is a necessary quality for democratic citizenship, according to our classic democratic theorists. Here again women score lower than men and again the differences are larger the lower the amount of formal education. Women on the grade-school level, where sex typing is most rigid, turn out to have the most impoverished level of political concept formation.

Two important consequences are likely to flow from this constellation of attitudes. The lesser involvement of women, the greater compliance with authority nurtured in them from childhood on, and the lesser sense of efficacy and political sophistication are bound to contribute to the *decline in issue-orientation and partisanship* among candidates for political offices. Our political dialogue in general will suffer. The stronger emphasis on moral issues among women, consonant with their approved "nurturant" roles, leads to excessive focus on the superficial and less relevant aspects of politics. In the opinion of some scholars, it is likely to breed somewhat greater intolerance and fear of conflict.[13]

To Thomas Jefferson, for one, nothing could be so disastrous for a democracy as a public obedient to authority and intolerant of those who challenged it. In the classic democratic image, voters are supposed to be informed, principled, and independent; at the same time, they must be guardful of the rights of minorities, no matter how hateful these may seem at particular times. When large segments of the population do not possess these characteristics, we are likely to be confronted with a latent protest vote of frightening dimensions, which, as professors John C. Livingston and Robert G. Thompson point out, "deter[s] leaders from publicly advocating or acting on their own convictions. . . ." The general result will be that "political leaders [will be] largely incapacitated from protecting the principles they are committed to and fail almost totally to challenge publicly the undemocratic views of a large segment of the electorate." [14] Such was, indeed, the case in the years of Senator Joseph McCarthy's witch-hunting craze. And if we are to trust the conclusion of Samuel Stouffer and his research staff, women at that time were beset with fears and motivated to crush radical dissent to an even *greater* extent than were men. Habitual compliance, passivity, and dependence are the very qualities we do not want in our citizens, according to classic democratic theories. If these attributes are combined with ignorance of democratic procedural values and confronted with complex and confusing crisis situations, it makes for a quite combustible mixture, as recent history has taught us. In the end, it is democracy itself that is threatened.

13. See, for example, Samuel Stouffer, *Communism, Conformity, and Civil Liberties* (Garden City, N.Y.: Doubleday, 1955), pp. 131–55; and David Riesman, "Orbits of Tolerance, Interviews and Elites," *Public Opinion Quarterly*, XX (1956), pp. 49–73.

14. John C. Livingston and Robert G. Thompson, *The Consent of the Governed* (New York: The Macmillan Co., 1966), p. 322.

II.

But then, women are not alone in being unable to measure up to the ideal of democratic citizenship posed by some of our forefathers. As voting analysis and opinion research has made abundantly clear, the American voter in general, male or female, falls far short of these standards. Issue-consciousness is limited to a small group of the population; there is widespread political apathy among many sectors of the public; and there is startlingly little understanding of democratic values and procedures.[15] Yet to pluralist theorists of democracy[16] this poses no great problem, for the system is saved by political elites who share a consensus on fundamental democratic values and who constitute the politically active and influential segment of the society. In *their* hands, democracy is safe. The competition between these elites ensures the citizens' right of participation; elite behavior can be influenced by making choices between competing elites in elections. Democratic values are affirmed also by the fact that these elites are not closed and that new groups can gain access to elite positions. Pluralists are sometimes accused of slighting the problem of political apathy and alienation and, equally, of denigrating the role of social movements and political radicals.[17] In the context of their explanatory scheme, it is a high degree of involvement and not apathy on the part of citizens that poses a problem. Given the lack of political sophistica-

15. See, for example, Campbell *et al., The American Voter*; and Stouffer, *Communism, Conformity, and Civil Liberties.* See also Herbert McClosky, "Consensus and Ideology in American Politics," *American Political Science Review* (June, 1964), pp. 361–82; and Lane, *Political Life.*

16. Foremost among these are Robert A. Dahl, Nelson Polsby, Charles Lindblom, and Aaron Wildavsky.

17. See, for example, Lane Davis, "The Cost of Realism: Contemporary Restatements of Democracy," *Western Political Quarterly,* XVII (1964), 37–46; Peter Bachrach and Morton S. Baratz, "The Two Faces of Power," *The American Political Science Review,* LVI (1962), 947–52; and Jack L. Walker, "A Critique of the Elitist Theory of Democracy," *The American Political Science Review,* II (1966), 285–96.

tion and appreciation of democratic values among Americans today, it is better that they stay quiescent and leave political involvement and governing to the elites.

To pluralists, consequently, the key problem in politics becomes that of *who governs?* Such is, indeed, the title of the most influential book coming out of this school.[18] The viability of pluralist democracy depends to a great extent on whether individuals fit to govern will be found in any situation. The successful politician, adept at negotiation and bargaining, can find formulas for compromise that will keep controversies from becoming too hot and conflict too divisive. This is crucial for the maintenance of stability and the preservation of democratic freedoms. But the individuals qualified to take on such delicate and difficult tasks are few and far between: one common estimate is that they amount to no more than about 2 percent of the population. And this tiny minority, on whom rests the responsibility of governing, must be constantly replenished.

Thus it would seem that the incapacities our sexist ideology aims to induce in half of our citizenry is a matter of grave concern for pluralist theories as well as for those of the classic democratic schools. We are being deprived, quite simply, of the potential political talents and skills to be found among these 53.7 percent of eligible voters. As long as sex standards and sex typing continue in their present forms, there is but little chance that women naturally endowed with the qualities needed for governing will be added to the pool of new recruits. This can only be viewed as a great loss, given the small dimensions and central importance of the latter. For pluralists and for classic democratic theorists alike, sexist ideology presents a formidable obstacle to the creation and/or maintenance of a viable democracy.

18. Robert Dahl, *Who Governs?* (New Haven: Yale University Press, 1961).

III.

The common ideal of manhood in America may also constitute a problem—at times a formidable one—to the pursuit of rational, cautious, and humane policies in this republic. Maleness, as defined by our sex standards, requires strength, daring, independence, and a certain brusqueness in tone and manner. This standard carries with it a tolerance and even admiration for physically aggressive behavior. Boys are usually encouraged to fight back—no matter what the odds; to accept defeat or to recognize one's weakness in a battle becomes very difficult for a young male socialized in our culture. Retreat in particular carries with it a social stigma that is painful to bear for the individual involved. The result appears to be that a good many American men suffer from what has been called the "John Wayne-syndrome"—the belief that a punch in the nose will set everything right! Although women, with their greater compliance with authority and attachment to the system and governmental figures, may be more prone to accept the conspiracy theories so frequently offered to explain away the problems of the nation, men, on the other hand, are likely to insist on pursuing policies shown to be unfruitful and even detrimental, on the basis of their fear of appearing weak or their distaste for retreating from a fight. Some rather astounding statements from contemporary leaders come to mind: President Lyndon B. Johnson, reacting to the Dominican revolt of 1965, refused to "sit in his rocking chair" and allow Communists to take over another country in Latin America—and so the Marines were sent in. President Nixon, in 1969, reacting to demands for a pull-out of American troops in Vietnam, refused to be the first American president in history to accept defeat in a battle we are involved in—and so the troops, at least most of them, stayed on. Senator Barry Goldwater, in commenting on negotiations with the Russians, wanted the president to speak with "the nukes [nuclear missiles] rattling in his pockets." Not to mention Senator Stennis, who professed no fear of a world nuclear disaster, as long as the new Adam and Eve be American.

What is peculiar and disturbing about such assertions is what they reveal about the motives guiding some of our leaders. Policies appear to be pursued not just for "reasons of state," but for reasons of *pride*—a pride that can come only from an acceptance of the ideals of manhood imposed upon us by sexist ideology. It is striking that even in the fall of 1970, with our Vietnam policy so evidently defunct, no less than 45 percent of American men were against the proposal to bring our troops home at the end of 1971. Among women, only 27 percent registered opposition to such a policy.[19] The sex gap shown by this poll is even greater than the one found at the time of the Korean War. Then, too, it was women more than men who wanted an end to the fighting—in spite of the fact that it was the men who were being killed. How else can we explain such proclivities than by recognizing that sex standards do not force *women* into the continued pursuit of policies associated with aggressiveness, determination, and presumed bravery —after these policies have proven fruitless and damaging to the nation and the world?

The point to be emphasized here is that the personality characteristics associated with proper femininity and manliness are arbitrarily assigned to each sex without regard to the very complex and wide-ranging differences inherent in the members of both. There are men who find it very difficult to be strong, independent, and aggressive, just as there are women who develop such attributes with comparative ease. But for either, the deviation from sex norms causes anxiety and severe emotional stress. One consequence of doubts or recognition of failure in the ability to live up to the approved sex standards of society is overcompensation in some area of behavior clearly associated in one's mind with what is typical of one's own sex. For men, this is more often than not aggressiveness. The "he-man" image—in mass media as well as literature—

19. Gallup poll testing the public's reaction to the Hatfield-McGovern plan to end U.S. troop involvement in Vietnam by the end of 1971. Reported in the *San Francisco Chronicle*, September 28, 1970, p. 11.

is that of the silent, strong men who can deal with recalcitrants and settle most problems through the application of physical force. The attitudes of men insecure in their feelings of "masculinity" are bound to be influenced by this incessant and excessive emphasis on aggressiveness in the male culture heroes. This may, indeed, go a long way towards explaining the prevalence of violence in American society—and the fact that by far most criminally violent behavior here is committed by men.

For women, compensation is likely to come in widely different aspects of behavior. Given the favored image of femininity flashed on screens and brandished in ads, where the female—whether as glamour girl or homemaker—orients her activities and her whole life around the man, a woman finding herself lacking in the supposed feminine attributes may make up for it by insisting, against all evidence, that she is only interested in loving and serving a man. Thus some women prominent in fields requiring just the assertiveness, ambition, and toughness that supposedly makes them inaccessible to females will declare that they are *really* just interested in making their men happy. Or women obviously dominant in a marriage or an erotic relationship will try to save their "femininity" by insisting that their only place is in the home. Again, we are reminded of some surprising statements by women who have attained fame and wealth at their own behest. Television personality Arlene Francis, for one, continuously fighting for a place in a field beset with difficulties and obstacles to women, still persisted for years in declaring that women were happiest and most fulfilled as housewives. Veteran actresses, like Rosalind Russell, in a profession that takes not just talent but usually both the keenest ambition and the rawest of guts, can often be heard declaring that they would gladly give it all up for the man of their choice anytime he asks for that. How lucky, then, that he doesn't—or that other reasons can be found for the divorces so common in the profession. Jacqueline Bisset, of recent movie fame, emphatically stated that what she really liked to do was cook and clean for her man. With an income of $100,000 or more yearly, her compelling need to do that can well be imagined. Shirley Temple Black, United

States representative to the United Nations in 1970 and for years active on her own in hard and bitterly fought political campaigns, declared while on a speaking tour in the fall of 1970 that she was not interested in "women's liberation"; she preferred the "protective arms of her husband" around her. Absenting herself from those as often as she does, she must be sorely bereaved indeed.

This is *not* just amusing. The psychological costs imposed by sexist ideology are difficult to bear for both men and women. The more rigid the sex typing and the more artificial the standards, the more the members of both sexes have to struggle with insecurities and guilt induced by traits and talents not compatible with what is expected of them. And the more stifled their potential and thwarted their development, the more frustrations and hidden resentments will come into play. The consequences—for individual as well as family happiness—can be devastating. For society, just as for democratic politics, the effect is clearly negative. A variety of social disturbances—neuroticism among housewives, criminal aggressiveness among males, rampant homosexuality, political apathy and rigidity in some sectors of the public—all can be traced to or are most likely associated with the impositions of sexist ideology. The nation loses a great deal, moreover, in the underutilization of its women in the political sector. And it loses most painfully in the poverty affecting self-supporting mothers and their children because of the gross inequities in pay and opportunities for women on the job market.

Special attention should be paid to the psychological burdens borne by men in a sexist society. As Dr. Joseph B. Furst points out, their greater freedom and opportunity are not unmixed blessings.[20] What it means in practice is that too much responsibility and too heavy burdens may be laid upon the man or assumed by him as a matter of course. The prescribed relationship between husband and wife calls for him to carry the entire financial burden of supporting a family. This often means that he cannot make himself break out of an occupation that he hates. If his wife has

20. Joseph B. Furst, *The Neurotic and His Inner and Outer Worlds* (New York: The Citadel Press, 1954), p. 87.

to work despite all of his efforts, he is likely to feel it as a terrible humiliation. A persistent anxiety will be present for the man with no guaranteed job security and a pervasive frustration for the many who continue at the treadmill while chafing at the bonds. A relaxation in sex standards, on the other hand, might permit men to encourage their wives to go to work when financial or personal needs call for it.

It is rather too much to bear for one individual to have to be ever supportive, resourceful, strong, and brave without showing signs of very human frailties and fears. The effect is often hostility to women and a rigidity of attitude and manners in erotic situations that gets in the way of love relationships. Sensitivity, tenderness, a willingness to fully share are *not* qualities often noted in the American man. Yet these are the qualities women seem to want, if we are to trust reports published by themselves and their analysts. Companionship and affection are more important than ever to marital happiness. But the man induced to accept "the cowboy syndrome" will be unable to fulfill the expectations of his wife.

What we are referring to here is the dominance of the "strong and silent" male model in our folk culture. As sociologist Charles W. Peck comments, John Wayne can't express his feelings toward women.[21] And James Bond doesn't have any. These are the two figures that have come to represent the male sex role in America. The consequences, Dr. Peck points out, are "a tragedy for American society."

It starts in the childhood of American males. When parents use the expression "he's all boy," what they mean is that he is aggressive, gets into trouble, or dirties himself. They never mean he is showing tenderness, emotion, or affection. "What parents are really telling their son is that a real man doesn't show his emotions and if he is a real man he won't allow his emotions to be expressed," says Dr. Peck. This is viewed as "a sign of femininity and undesirable for a male." The result is that the male child grows up to be tongue-tied like John Wayne or unfeeling like James Bond. Both types treat women "with an air of emotional detachment

21. Quoted in the *San Francisco Chronicle*, September 20, 1970, p. 9.

and independence." The playboy looks at sex as a packageable product; the woman in the process is reduced to a playboy accessory. The cowboy *feels,* all right—he loves his woman and his horse (or in the modern day version, his car) equally, but the expression of such feeling would conflict with his image of masculinity.

What happens when either of the two characters marries can easily be imagined. And the situation is not improved where a woman who has no special capacity for love is put in a position where she has nothing to do but love, as Vivian Gornick points out in the *Village Voice.* The result is that the modern American woman seeks to drive and dominate both her husband and her children. Says Miss Gornick:

> She displays an aberrated, aggressive ambition for her mate and her offspring, which can be explained only by the most vicious feelings toward the self. The reasons are obvious. The woman who must love for a living, the woman who has no self, no objective external reality to take her own measure by, no work to discipline her, no goal to provide the illusion of progress, no separate mental existence, is constitutionally incapable of the emotional distance that is one of the real requirements for love.[22]

Sexism does, indeed, have many and varied victims.

IV.

In his brilliant analysis of American democracy, *The Semi-Sovereign People,* E. E. Schattschneider concludes that the unused political potential in the United States could change the whole balance of power in the system. It is, in his comment, "sufficient to blow the United States off the face of the earth." [23]

What Schattschneider is referring to are the roughly 40 million

22. Quoted in the *Sacramento Bee,* March 13, 1970, p. B3.
23. E. E. Schattschneider, *The Semi-Sovereign People* (New York: Holt, Rinehart and Winston, 1969), p. 99.

adult citizens who do not vote in presidential elections (37.6 million in 1968). That is really "a stupendous segment of the nation" blocked out from the political system.[24] What makes it even more important is that their disfranchisement has been accomplished by extra-legal means. It seems, in fact, to be voluntary. We have to worry about these 40 million adult Americans who seem to be "so unresponsive to the regime that they do not trouble to vote." To Schattschneider, their nonvoting makes a crucial difference: First, because "anything that looks like a rejection of the political system by so large a fraction of the population is a matter of great importance. Second, anything that looks like a limitation of the expanding universe of politics is certain to have great practical consequences." [25]

In the presidential election of 1968 there were more than 21 million women among the 37.5 million nonvoters. To get at the *practical* consequences flowing from their abstention from the polls, we have to do more than count numbers. We have to examine the social structure of the disfranchised, Schattschneider suggests. And if we are to get at the relationship of *sexist ideology* to the results obtained, we have to find the differences in turnout proportions between the sexes by geographical area, type of community, and level of education, for we know already that sex standards and sex typing are the most rigid in the South, in village and rural areas, and among people on lower educational levels.

But first, who are the nonvoters generally? And how would our political system change if they were to suddenly invade it? As Schattschneider points out, "every study of the subject supports the conclusion that nonvoting is a characteristic of the poorest, least well-established, least educated stratum of the community." [26] We cannot, therefore, take it for granted that the 37.5 million or so abstainers would be divided along the conservative-liberal-radical spectrum in the same proportion as the 67.8 million who are now

24. Ibid., p. 97.
25. Ibid., p. 99.
26. Ibid., p. 105.

participants in the system. It is more likely that they would line up behind programs and candidates that would improve and expand the welfare state, end poverty, and bring forth a greater measure of social justice and economic security for the common citizen. Self-interest is, after all, a strong and reasonably steady factor in voting behavior. "False consciousness" and the tendency to go with obvious public favorites may enter into and distort the picture somewhat,[27] but in general, one can argue as the late authority V. O. Key did, that "voters are not fools—in the large the electorate behaves about as rationally and responsibly as we should expect given the clarity of the alternatives presented to it and the character of the information available to it." [28] Schattschneider concurs: The present cleavages tend to freeze the stakes of politics at a point that has never involved the whole community. ". . . The root of the problem of nonvoting is to be found in the way in which the alternatives in American politics are defined, the way in which issues get referred to the public, the scale of competition and organization, and above all *what* issues are developed." [29]

It is, of course, a two-way flow. Citizens stay away from the polls primarily because politics does not seem to relate to their needs. And politicians, on the other hand, refrain from developing and pursuing issues that do not seem to have much relevance to the citizens presently active in the political system. As a consequence, "a multitude of causes languish because the 40 million or so nonvoters do not support them at the polls." What would happen if they inter-

27. It is, for instance, well established that members of the working class favor the Democratic party, looked to as the sponsor of welfare programs, while middle- and upper-class groups favor Republicans. See, for example, S. M. Lipset, *Political Man* (New York: Doubleday, 1959). On the other hand, a "psychological bandwagon effect," discovered in the elections of 1952 and 1956, where General Eisenhower was a heavy public favorite, indicates that on such occasions the general Democratic preference of nonvoters is likely to be unreliable. See Angus Campbell *et al.*, "Voting Turnout," in Norman R. Lutbeg, ed., *Public Opinion and Public Policy* (Homewood, Ill.: The Dorsey Press, 1968), pp. 46–58.

28. V. O. Key, *The Responsible Electorate* (Cambridge: Harvard University Press, 1966), p. 7.

29. Schattschneider, *The Semi-Sovereign People*, p. 110.

vened staggers the imagination. "All political equations would be revised." [30]

So it is those on the bottom of the social order who stand to gain the most from an expansion of the popular base of political participation. To anyone who agrees with Schattschneider that a special sensitivity to *their* needs and experiences is one of the great moral claims of democracy as a system, it becomes vitally important to eradicate the causes for nonparticipation—to the extent, at least, that it leads to certain social issues being defined out of politics. The cause *we* are interested in, the ideology of sexism, appears to be responsible for the absence of more than 4.5 million potential votes in the last election, for this is the difference in turnout between men and women at that time. We need not for the moment touch on the problem of expanding the scope of the political system in general. Let us, then, look at the possible impact these 4.5 million votes might have on the political scene today.

To verify our hypothesis concerning the relationship between social structure and sexist ideology to nonvoting among women, let us take a closer look at the data. There may, to be sure, be a variety of reasons for women not going to the polls. Beyond the reasons that are common to both sexes, child-care responsibilities are the most likely obstacle, yet researchers found this to make little difference in voting turnout. Childless women in the South and childless women of grade-school education vote less frequently than men in the same categories. Also, this presumed barrier is not present for older women, yet sex differences in voting turnout do not diminish accordingly in this case either.[31]

As the Survey Research Center's team found out, it is *where* women live and *how much education* they have absorbed that more than anything else influences their participation in politics. Table 7.1 of our study pointed to some of these factors. Tables 7.2 and 7.3 will make the picture even clearer. Outside of the South, sex differences averaged across three categories of age and the two lower educa-

30. Ibid., pp. 110–11.
31. Campbell *et al., The American Voter,* pp. 487–88.

Table 7.2

RELATION OF SEX, EDUCATION,
AND REGION TO POLITICAL INVOLVEMENT*

	Men			Women		
	Grade School	*High School*	*College*	*Grade School*	*High School*	*College*
Non-South						
High involvement	27%	36%	49%	19%	30%	46%
Medium involvement	36	45	41	34	46	46
Low involvement	37	19	10	47	24	8
	100%	100%	100%	100%	100%	100%
Number of cases	387	494	219	399	719	186
South						
High involvement	29%	33%	38%	14%	25%	57%
Medium involvement	32	39	49	33	41	35
Low involvement	39	28	13	53	34	8
	100%	100%	100%	100%	100%	100%
Number of cases	187	146	77	217	232	83

Source: Angus Campbell, Philip E. Converse, Warren E. Miller, and Donald E. Stokes,
The American Voter *(Ann Arbor, Mich.: Survey Research Center, University of Michigan,*
1960), p. 490. Reprinted by permission of the Survey Research Center.

* Figures in this table are based on a combination of data from the 1952 and 1956
election samples.

tion groupings within type of residence. As pointed out earlier, it is
in the areas where sex typing generally is most rigid that the differences show up.

The conclusion drawn by the scholars responsible for *The American Voter* parallels our own. According to them, it is "vestigial sex
roles" that make for the basic differences in the political participa-

Table 7.3

AVERAGE DIFFERENCES
IN TURNOUT PROPORTIONS OF THE SEXES

	Metropolitan	+5%
Non-South	City and town	+20%
	Village and rural	+28%

*Source: Angus Campbell, Philip E. Converse, Warren
E. Miller, and Donald E. Stokes, The American
Voter (Ann Arbor, Mich.: Survey Research Center,
University of Michigan, 1960), p. 487. Reprinted by
permission of the Survey Research Center.*

tion of men and women,[32] "vestigial" because the granting of suffrage
to women implies a shift in former role definitions, where the man
was the political agent for the family unit and the woman was not
to concern herself with politics. As we have seen, however, these
vestiges of political patriarchy are too prominent and influential to
be taken lightly. They would seem to be responsible for no less than
4.5 million votes lost to the nation in the presidential election of
1968, this being the number of women nonvoters over men nonvoters. Unless, of course, the cleavages among these nonparticipants
were to correspond to those existing among the voters, this could
make for a very different outcome in the election and a very different outcome in policy formulation and output by the officials elected.

Let us remember that the election was decided with a small differential of votes in favor of the Republican presidential candidate.
Let us also keep in mind that the nonvoters, *in particular* the
women nonvoters, are by and large on the lower socioeconomic
levels. Residence in rural areas and in the South and lower educational levels, primary factors in the explanation of greater ratios of
nonvoting among women, are equally factors pointing to the likelihood of this group being on the bottom of the social barrel. Given,
then, the usual preference for the Democratic party among citizens
in the "out-groups" of society, it seems clear that the invasion of these

32. Ibid., p. 484.

4.5 million women into the political system would at the very least have ensured the election of a Democratic administration. One may hypothesize, of course, that a portion of their votes would have gone to presidential candidate George Wallace, but given the much greater preference for peace programs and proposals found among women, it is likely that the blatantly hawkish tone of his campaign would have turned a great many of them off. The Democratic party or very socially oriented and progressive candidates of the Republican party should, then, get the support of this group. Its needs are, by and large, for programs and policies to upgrade the quality of life for those living on the poverty or "economy" level in our society. Insofar as the presidential election itself is concerned, there is little doubt that their use of the vote would win the day for the Democratic presidential candidate.

That in itself carries quite an impact on the political and social scene of America. The central position of the presidency in the system is, as noted earlier, recognized by everyone. Although the two major parties in recent decades have tended to come closer in programs and policies, the difference in emphasis on the need to eradicate poverty, to channel funds into higher education, and to support civil rights programs have emerged as significant, particularly in the first years of the Nixon administration. A Democratic administration would be honor-bound to try to keep the unemployment rate down, and equally, to continue programs aimed at aiding the "out-groups" in American society. With an influx of, say, at least 3 to 3.5 million supporters on the lower socioeconomic levels, the liberals of the party would be in a stronger position to push the kind of policies traditionally favored by their sector. What that could mean, in the end, would be a genuine welfare state with a certain level of economic security, full medical care, and educational opportunities guaranteed to every citizen.

An expansion of the effective political community would quite simply mean new and greater emphasis on the options and alternatives that reflect the needs of the present nonparticipants. The impact of the newcomers should quickly make itself felt within the

Republican party as well. If cleavages within the body of voters now active in the system do not change, this party, too, would have to move in the direction of liberalization in the socioeconomic sphere, if it is to win in future national elections. Registration is already in the favor of the Democrats; the margin of victory for Republican candidates is generally very small, and the Goldwater-Johnson contest in 1964 offered convincing evidence that even without the influx of several million new voters on lower socioeconomic levels, there is a decisive trend against the type of candidates and platforms that promise a halt or turning back of welfare programs now in existence. Barring intervening issues carrying great and unusual emotional loads, a true conservative cannot be elected on the national level at least.

Another important result to be obtained from the projected expansion of the effective electorate if sexist ideology were to lose its hold would be a gradual diminution in the now shocking dimension of the nonvoting sector of the American polity, both male and female, since new policies would better relate to their needs. Their current abstention reflects nothing so much as the fact that conflicts now familiar to American politics have little relevance for them. But as both parties go after the 4.5 million women voters who are now held back mainly by "vestigial" sex roles, they will have to, given the usual income and status of these women, raise issues and make proposals that bear on the fates of nonvoters of both sexes. As a consequence, a different organization of politics should ensue, bringing us closer to a nationalization of politics where "competing leaders and organizations define the alternatives of public policy in such a way that the public can participate in the decision-making process." [33]

Such is Schattschneider's *operational* definition of democracy. We cannot think of a better one. Whether it fits the American system as now organized is quite another question. Even the most eloquent and perceptive defender of our political order, Robert Dahl, agrees that the rates of political participation that have been characteristic

33. Schattschneider, *The Semi-Sovereign People*, p. 141.

of this citizen body are "deplorably low." [34] An expansion in the scope of the political community is essential whatever one's conception of democracy. In our preferred order, there simply is no room for *a silenced majority*.

34. Robert A. Dahl, "Further Reflections on the Elitist Theory of Democracy," *The American Political Science Review*, II (June, 1966), 301.

Eight

THE LIBERATED SOCIETY

Vision and Strategies

What does woman want? Or—what does woman need?

At this point in time the two questions are likely to bring forth quite different responses. Given the impact and pervasiveness of sexist ideology, one cannot expect that the majority of American women will express any interest in changing the traditional role and place of woman in this society. But reformers and rebels have never waited for the masses to give approval for them to go ahead in their drive to free humans from their shackles. It would be a much sadder and poorer world, indeed, if they did. Instead, they allow normative ideals, a vision of a better future, and faith in the possibility of change to guide their action. And, at times, they have been proven right. It would be hard to argue—with *some* knowledge of human history—that either change or improvements in the human condition are impossible. Certainly, the "heroes of history" never heeded the advice of the pessimists. As single-minded as they were passionate, they forged ahead in their reformatory or revolutionary drives no matter how few their followers or how great the obstacles at the start. More often than not, history confirms the truth in the old maxim: "There is no stopping of an idea whose time has come."

So it may be with the new feminism in America. Since it is based on the belief that women are *humans* entitled to the same opportunities for self-expression as men, the question for the movement is *not* what women want as of the present, but *what women need* to become free and fully realized individuals. No false theories of woman's nature, no ideologically based view of her proper role in society, no artificial sex norms can be allowed to stand in the way of the human development of the female. Equality of education, equality of opportunity, equality of income and status on a par with men are but the most basic and immediate demands of the new feminists. Beyond that, the true liberation of the American woman requires a society structured quite differently than America is right now. What is needed is a society where arrangements are made to ensure the realization and utilization of the potential of *every* human being, for there are too many men among us whose talents remain undeveloped, whose skills are not used, whose spirits are still twisted. To simply aspire to *their* current status and position, therefore, although it would imply a significant improvement in the lot of women, cannot in the long run satisfy the variety of needs and interests suppressed for thousands of years. Women have had to wait too long and male domination has been too complete for the reforms in question to accomplish the transformation of both life style and quality of life envisioned by most feminists. Their aspirations and needs will necessitate far-reaching and profound change, change that cannot help but free the men of America, as well. The liberation of women will mean—*must* mean—the liberation of men.

I.

Let us reflect on the character and qualities of a society where both sexes are allowed a full and free flowering of talents and a choice of work and life style that is in line with their temperament and desires. This would have to be a society where sex norms were concerned with maintaining the dignity of individuals and essential decency and sensitivity in a sexual union. No more. Each person could be herself or himself—emotional, rational, assertive, quiet, strong, or weak—without fear of violating sex standards and dangerously straying from the approved sex typing. A young man might cry at movies, write poetry, dance ballet, or enjoy feeding and caring for a family without crushing the fears and doubts about his manhood now forced upon him by sexist ideology. A young woman might decide that she loves the rough and tumble of politics, the daring pursuit of, say, race-driving, or the serious and dedicated work of scientists, and she might freely be assertive, competitive, and dominant socially or at work, without the gnawing doubts and cruel put-downs now common for such "unfeminine behavior. In their relationships with one another, people could equally transcend the stereotyping we know only too well. *She* might at times take the initiative for both social engagements and sexual encounters; he just possibly might enjoy being the one pursued, the more passive partner. More importantly, they could be companions and friends, not just husband and wife, not just sexual beings seeking from each other a hard-won gratification of both ego and physical desires. Creativity, sharing, and joy in a sexual union could be possible as both partners developed a clear concept of self and were free from the rigidities of sex typing and the sex norms.

In such a society, the family could take a variety of forms. It is a fair bet that it will be with us for quite some time yet, but a relaxation in its role structure and experimentation with its form is bound to come. No longer need the only fully approved family unit be the one where father is the breadwinner, mother the housewife, and Mary and Joe the overprotected, TV-dazed little kids dividing their time between neighborhood school and cozy suburban homestead. There can instead be a variety of options for the activities and life style of all family members. In the family that stayed nuclear in form, the mother in our liberated society would have a chance to take on the work of her choice, and that would include, of course, the chance to stay on as a housewife. Only this time, her work would be socially valued, with the usual guarantees of time off, vacation, and pension upon retirement. If she decided to join the labor force outside, there would be attractive, secure, and well-staffed child-care centers available for the children. And when she came home, then, from her outside job, both she and the father—possibly the children, too—would share in the care and maintenance of family and home, freeing her to be a true companion and friend to all. The father, equally, would have more options available to him. He might choose to stay home or to experiment in a variety of occupations, secure in the knowledge that the financial responsibility was no longer his alone and that no one would ever question his manhood on the basis of his preferences in work or social life.

But the nuclear family might no longer fill the needs of a good number of individuals. A communal arrangement or an extended family would offer to many a greater flexibility and freedom, without in any way diminishing the sense and experience of sharing and responsibility. Such experimental units are, in fact, quite in vogue today among groups of younger people. The possibilities here are exciting, but, unquestionably, present sexual mores get in the way of building the kind of commune that would free women from their stereotyped menial assignments—or from sexual exploitation. The answer is *not* the super-sexed group life carried to nightmarish dimensions by the Charlie Manson "family." What is happening here is simply that a woman is expected to have sexual relations with any man who wants to, without regard to *her* inclinations and taste at the moment. Neither is the answer the kind of back-to-nature, "hip" communes where women still end up doing their "womanly" things and where the cleaning, scrubbing, and cooking are only more arduous, servile, and backbreaking than back in the much-suspected consumer culture. No, and emphatically no. In a liberated society such cultural throwbacks would get only the contempt and ridicule they deserve. For communes to be genuine communities, sharing of responsibilities, decisions, and pleasures would *not* take place in accordance with sex divisions.

The greatest advantage offered by an extended family is that children would be freed from the sometimes suffocatingly close atmosphere of suburban home life and would learn to know and live with a variety of people of many ages, backgrounds, and personalities. The children would learn to take on responsibilities for themselves and others; egotism and a keen sense of possession would be discouraged, since trust and sharing are the qualities needed and fostered by such living arrangements. The greater and more varied exposure to other humans, the feeling of brotherhood and common purpose known to the best of such families, could not help but make children both happier and more humanly decent individuals. Responsiveness and responsibility would replace the dependence and selfishness found in many children subject to the excessive mothering of an omnipresent mother and the occasional, exasperated attention of a much-harassed father. We have, in fact, much evidence on hand that the children raised in the kibbutzes of Israel or in the child-care centers of Scandinavia and the Soviet Union are both mentally more healthy and happier than the majority of American children today.[1]

Joy could come back to marriage and interest be added to ongoing relationships when the union of man and woman implied an enlargement of the life experiences for both and not the sudden withdrawal and exclusive focus on home and marriage for her. A woman could seek a mate and eventually children only when she truly desired this experience. There would be no more social pressure and snickering contempt for the woman who did not marry. The relief for the man should be considerable; the groom who tries escape outside the church door is so common a figure in our folklore that it testifies to widespread resentment of the pressures and manipulation trapping *him* as well. Fatherhood, like motherhood, would be a question of free and thoughtful choice. Children would not be brought into the world because of infantile fantasies about cute, cuddly babies bringing feminine fulfillment or adding decor to the home scene. Nor would they be fathered because of deep-rooted insecurities and half-crazed drives to prove one's masculinity or add status through the acquisition of offspring. In our liberated society, the educational experiences and the mass culture would not force on

1. See, for example, the overview of several studies in David Rapaport, "The Study of Kibbutz Education and Its Bearing on the Theory of Development," *American Journal of Orthopsychiatry*, XXVIII (1958), 587–99; Bruno Bettelheim, "Growing Up Female," *Harper's*, October, 1962; Jane Whitbreak, "A New Way to Raise Kids," *Look*, February 24, 1970, pp. 64–68; Urie Brontenbreuner, *Two Worlds of Childhood* (New York: Russel Sage Foundation, 1970); and the discussion in Alice S. Rossi, "Inequality between the Sexes," in R. J. Lifton, ed., *The Woman in America* (Boston: Houghton Mifflin Co., 1964), pp. 106–19.

men and women such conflicting needs and divisive experiences. Both would be reared as individuals, with talents and temperaments specific to the *person*, not to the *sex;* and both would learn self-reliance, responsibility, and self-respect as they grew and developed. Cooperation, spiritual union, excitement in sexual relations could then take the place of debilitating suspicions and the terrible hostility now so familiar between the sexes. Both everyday behavior and common and high-brow culture testify to the presence of latent but intense sexual resentments and "impotent rage," to use Betty Friedan's term. It is remarkable, as she has pointed out, that all a popular comedian has to do to start his audience tittering and guffawing is to come out on stage and say two words: "My wife. . . ." [2] Yet as women are liberated the sex war in America *can* come to an end, as indeed it *must* before it does further damage to relationships and the quality of social and political life in general.

II.

Concretely, what such a society demands is a variety of institutional innovations and a complete reordering of economic priorities. The current platforms of women's rights groups offer a good *start*, but *no more than that*, in policy proposals called for to bring about a sexually liberated society. The demands by now include equal pay and equal opportunities, paid maternity leaves with guarantees for women to return to their jobs, well-staffed and sound child-care centers in the communities or at the places of employment, elimination of abortion laws, pensions and severance pay for housewives, and an end to all discriminatory practices both on the job and in public accommodations, to be ensured, preferably, by the enactment of the Equal Rights Amendment. To this list must be added the very important request that the image of women in the mass media and in children's textbooks be changed. Women must be portrayed as some-

2. Speech delivered at Sacramento State College, October 8, 1970.

thing else and something more than brainless sexpots or possessive and spiritually diminished house slaves.

Can even these demands be accommodated within the present political and economic structures? To some extent, yes; in some respects, no. They will, in the first place, require far greater public expenditures than are now afforded social programs in this society. On the other hand, child-care centers, housewives' pensions, equal-pay arrangements, and free abortions, are all policies already in effect in a number of societies with a proportionately far lower GNP than we have in the United States. The Soviet Union and the socialist countries in general, and with a few exceptions, West Germany, the Scandinavian countries, and England, are all pledged to and on the way to implementing such programs, if they are not already in full operation.[3]

Given these latter examples, it is clear that the capitalist system need not be totally transformed in order to introduce the reforms in question. Neither will the present feminist demands impose impossible burdens on the economy. They will, however, require a substantial reshuffling of budgetary expenditures, as well as the acceptance of new tasks of social responsibility on the part of industry and institutions of higher education. Child-care centers at the place of work or study, paid maternal leaves, and equal pay are innovations that will not come cheaply to the employers and institutions with whom women are involved today. For the small-scale ones, governmental subsidies may be necessary. But for the rest, both the general rate of profits taken in yearly and the very great earnings derived over the years from the sex discrimination should make sufficient provisions for the institution of these reforms.

A warning must be issued at this point, lest it be thought that the road ahead will be an *easy* one to travel. The programs outlined will not be adopted by the mere appeal to the common sense and humani-

3. Norway, Denmark, and England have yet to enact legislation for house-wives' pensions or severance pay. In the Scandinavian countries and West Germany, abortion is free, that is, it is paid for through the system of government-insured medical care, but cannot be had at the request of the mother-to-be. Doctors have to agree that abortion is socially or medically necessary.

tarian instincts of business elites, administrators, and lawmakers. *Political pressures* will have to be applied at all points; confrontation politics in many instances will gradually have to be combined with the thrust of organized groups of women and their allies working either with or against selected power-wielders. It is likely to be a painful and sometimes violent process—as is any process of far-reaching system-wide change. But the weapons of the "out-group" in American society—the sit-in demonstrations, the boycotts, the slow-down strikes, the electioneering—are available to women no less than they have been available in the past to workers and to ethnic minorities, and, with the added advantages of potentially greater numbers and multiple political coalitions at a time of renewed social awakening and ferment, the chances are for women to succeed where other minorities have failed. Given political awareness and given group cohesion among a substantial number of women, a *movement* can be built, a movement strong enough to force the changes in question. Public harassment, financial injury, and the unseating of political officeholders are formidable weapons in the hands of determined and well-organized groups in a democracy. And these are *all* weapons available to women, who can use them with the *added* punch of hands presumed to be weaker and accustomed only to rocking the cradle. The vision of having patrols of heavily armed policemen or National Guardsmen with rifles and/or bayonets descending on crowds of American mothers assembled to demonstrate for equal rights might be enough to send lawmakers shuddering to their assemblies to vote for at least the *minimal* requests issued.

In dealing with business elites who refuse to treat women employees fairly or who persistently resist the feminists' demands for child-care centers, paid maternal leaves, and the like, the weapon of the *consumer boycott* could be supremely effective as the movement comes to encompass larger numbers. Slowdown strikes by female workers, public demonstrations, and sit-ins aimed at exposing the company's recalcitrance and injustices are likely to bring forth at the same time both the wholesale wrath of the establishment against the activists and the very changes sought. Few businesses can afford the damage to their prestige and the consequent financial loss involved by deliberately alienating a substantial group of citizens. To break down prolonged resistance among certain business elites, the government will have to be involved. But the threat of cut-offs of government contracts or subsidies is frequently sufficient to make corporation executives accept and even take the initiative to institute new programs and rules.

Ultimately, the government must be made the ally of women in their quest for equality and liberation. Beyond adopting and implementing legislation to insure equity and opportunities for women in education and on the job market, it is to governmental sources one will have to look for the financing of a major portion of the feminist program. Housewives' pensions, opportunities for free abortion, the re-education of women necessary to create a true measure of equality of opportunity, as well as the rewriting of public textbooks and the initiation of course programs on women all have to be funded by government on various levels. The problem of *how* to make government the ally in this enterprise is basically that of how to awaken the political consciousness of women and to create the conditions conducive to a political thrust. A variety of examples from the past suggest that forceful pressure groups, strong electoral minorities, or—as in this case—a potential electoral majority can force surprising changes upon both "king-makers" and lawmakers in a democracy. We shall discuss the problem of creating political awareness at some length later in this chapter. Before we go on, however, the *money question* has to be attended to. Quite simply, where is it going to come from, given the already excessive demands on the budget, both on the federal and state level, and the very heavy tax burdens imposed on the average citizen today?

There is no holy order, no unconquerable spirit that decrees that our *budgetary priorities* shall continue to be what they are at present. Women can and will have to question the propriety of having 70 percent of federal budgetary outlays go to "defense needs." It is a fair bet that they will be joined in making that challenge by a sizable number of men. With the war in Southeast Asia coming to an end and the reported need for American troops in Europe and elsewhere less and less convincing, chances appear quite good for a reordering of governmental priorities, a reordering essential for even the minimal demands of feminists to be met. It will, of course, require political action—by and on behalf of women and other "outgroups" in American society. This has already started. The present plight of large numbers of workers and defense experts suddenly left without jobs, is likely, if anything, to add momentum to the drive for de-emphasis on defense and re-emphasis on social programs.

The point to be made here is: *It can be done*. The feminist program, as outlined here, can be enacted without too much straining or radical transformation of the present economic structures. What we have talked about so far are reforms and innovations common to democratic welfare states as well as socialist states; and what has happened in the former confirms the judgment of many economists that the capitalist order is more flexible and durable than earlier suspected. An overthrow of the system is as unlikely as it is unnecessary for the eradication of the most overt of institutionally sanctioned sexist behavior. What will be required, however, is a serious modification towards a more mixed economy, where the government takes on new responsibilities and new authority vis-à-vis corporate elites and where women and their allies are in the position vis-à-vis government of demanding far greater accountability and responsiveness to their needs.

What makes such changes possible and even likely in our time are a few prominent developments of a social, political, and economic nature that tend to converge and thereby to confirm the historic invincibility of the feminist idea in this period. Economically, we have come to the point in our society where the problem is no longer to increase production generally in order to create *new* surplus capital for the upgrading of life among the present underprivileged group. For that, all we need is a more fair and equitable distributive system and a rechanneling of expenditures on the governmental level. Our productive apparatus is, in fact, capable of putting out all the goods necessary to ensure the material well-being of every American alive, and then with some surplus to spare. Ordinarily— that is, in peacetime—our productive apparatus generally operates at about 60 percent capacity, for the simple reason that not enough income has been generated among American consumers to avail themselves of the products and inventions the market so easily may offer. This is not to suggest that what we need in this country is more consumerism among those already affluent. We may, on the contrary, need less—a shift in emphasis as to socially valued goods among these groups is highly desirable from the point of view of anyone concerned with human and not just materialistic values. We do, however, have among us about 45 million people living in poverty or in "near" poverty[4] and this one-fourth to one-fifth of our nation can surely use more and better housing, clothing, and nutrition, all of which can be made available to them by merely utilizing the presently unused portion of our productive apparatus. Beyond that, we can *all* use better schools, more hospitals, improved recreation facilities, cleaner air and water.

What is so striking about this great accumulation of pressing public needs is that they occur at a time when the problem for our manufacturers is not the ability to expand production facilities and rates, but rather *where* to channel surplus capital and *how* to prevent constriction due to the inability of the consuming public to absorb what they can offer. If part of that surplus capital were redirected to the public in the form of a greater share of the profits to the employees and to the public coffers for the purpose of meeting social needs, then both our corporate economy and the public sector could flourish. Clearly, the expansion required to meet these needs cannot now come in the defense sector. Since this industry is already overdeveloped, technological trends and innovations have meant that even the most extravagant new programs, such as space exploration, will employ relatively few of the best trained and most highly educated. The employment picture generally will not improve; the great public expenditures will not be "spread around." And it is that "spreading around" that we now have an imperative need for.

Consequently, as these facts become known and are absorbed by politically active groups among the public, pressures may be applied

4. The total of poor and near poor was estimated at 47 million in 1966 by Senator Paul Douglas. See Paul Douglas, *In Our Time* (New York: Harcourt, Brace & World, 1968), p. 129.

towards government to make the necessary changes in both the taxa-
tion system and the budget to improve our public life and our
economy. Corporation elites will resist, to be sure, since the
changes suggested will cut into their overall rate of profits and partially into their rights to make decisions not in line with public needs.
In the long run, however, it is in their own enlightened self-interest
to go along with such reforms—as corporation elites in Western
Europe have come to discover, a mixed economy and expanded welfare state are both inevitable and beneficial for their own overall
interests.

This is why the economic part of feminist demands can and will
be met, provided there is the kind of political awakening and thrust
always needed to get democratic government off a dead end and start
it moving in new directions. Socially and politically, the time is ripe
as well for activists in the feminist and progressive camps to gain
in their advances—socially because the myth of "capitalism for the
workers" is gradually being exposed as the sham it is, with the lack of
job security and the vagaries of the stock market most often hitting
the little guy, as dramatically evidenced in recent years; socially also
because of the growing awareness of a multitude of social needs and
the increasing tendency to look to government to meet them; politically because the prominent egalitarian strain in American political
thought makes for a likely acceptance of the moral basis for the
feminist claims; and politically also because the ground has been
prepared, so to speak, for reformers' drives and activists' thrusts by
the multitude of radical challenges hurled at "the establishment" in
recent years. The most promising of all factors is to be found in the
statistics—the fact that women constitute 53.7 percent of all Americans eligible to vote (as of 1968).

One cannot deny the possibility of intervening issues taking prece-
dence for a while. Campus revolts and terrorism by extremists of
both radical and reactionary persuasions may bring about a backlash reaction among the public and a crackdown by government
authorities that will make any new action and organizing nearly
impossible for a period. But the question of "Can it happen here?"
should not be allowed to interfere with either visions or plans for

a better future. If it happens, then everything may be in vain. To let that frightening eventuality get in the way of needed actions would surely just contribute to its realization.

Beyond all this, beyond the envisioned enactment of the present feminist program, it must again be recognized that *further reforms* are required for a decent and creative life to be possible for all Americans. The greater infusion of women in the work force, for example, will necessitate fewer work hours daily or a shorter work week for all. Housing patterns may have to be changed as it becomes more common for both parents to work: the isolation and heavy commuting connected with suburbia should be replaced with communities where work, social activities, and family life can be more easily and pleasurably integrated. Vacations must be extended for both parents. Both family and personal needs and contemporary practices call for an urgent revision of the current American vacation pattern. (Many technologically advanced societies offer all workers one month of paid vacation yearly, none offer less than three weeks.) If abortion laws are to be liberalized and abortions essentially financed through government agencies, medical care for both sexes is due for a similar general reorganization. And if women are to be given the chance to get all the educational and occupational opportunities their talents and efforts prove them to be suited for, then men too require the same for themselves. The educational apparatus, consequently, will have to be expanded, with access and finances guaranteed to everyone qualified. The job market, too, will require expansion, with a far greater emphasis on the utilization of all talents and much more room for experimentation.

It may be that the enactment of far-reaching programs such as these require in the end not just a modification, but a whole transformation of the present economic structure. But then we are greatly aided by the fact that both our ethical principles and industrial needs press precisely towards a greater egalitarianism. It is a major theme both in the American creed and in Western philosophy and ethics generally that all humans have a right to an equal opportunity. That can only mean, in the context of our time, that as children and young people they be provided with *all* they need to *learn* and to *develop*—which includes not only schooling, but also decent housing, clothing, and nutrition. It also means, as William J. Goode points out, that talent may be found in any segment of the society and that when education transforms talent into skill this should be put to use.[5]

The time has come then for the feminist ideas, the feminist program, and all that it implies to sweep to the forefront and gradually gain acceptance—not just by women, but by everyone with an interest in the future of this nation.

III.

What immediately lies ahead, however, is conflict, turmoil, hostile reactions, and possibly even violence, as the new feminist movement surges ahead to boldly challenge tradition-mired sexist practices. It is likely to be an uphill battle for quite a while. Far more than boldness will be required to carry the charge of this feminist brigade. The movement at present is split into several groups, each to some extent going its own way. Working women, middle-class married women, and students bring quite different kinds of interests and perspectives to the struggle. Yet whether it is economic oppression, psychological mutilation, or sexual exploitation that is foremost on the minds of members of each group, the aim for all is to end the total institutionalized oppression of women in this society. The basis for unity is there—across race and class lines— for every woman today knows and has to deal with discrimination and exploitation in one or another of these spheres. Women's liberation consequently has the potential of becoming the most broadly based and politically potent social movement of America in the seventies and eighties.

It is crucial that strategy for the various groups involved be developed out of the most incisive and honest analysis of their political positions at present. The most essential facts to be considered

5. William J. Goode, *World Revolution and Family Patterns* (Englewood Cliffs, N.J.: Prentice-Hall, Inc., 1964).

may be these: Women constitute a majority of this nation; the majority of women are at this time opposed to the movement; institutional power is almost entirely in the hands of men; and women have common cause in many instances with significant groups of men.

The most immediate problem for this, as for all burgeoning social movements, is how to move from a situation of apathy, alienation, and weakness to one of awareness, unity, and strength.

In the light of our analysis, *changing the consciousness of women* should be on the first order of priority. Until that happens, women cannot be organized in substantial enough numbers to change the sexist structure of this society. And genuine liberation, in all spheres of life, can only come with such structural change.

Changing the consciousness of women is, however, an immensely difficult task, given the resources of the movement at this time. To do that effectively, feminists should have use of the media; they should have influence and/or authority in the educational apparatus, the churches, and the advertising industry, to name but the most important opinion-molding institutions in America. As we know only too well by now, women are almost totally removed from positions of authority or significant influence in these structures. Feminists are, in fact, in the position that the civil rights movement found itself in in the early sixties when SNCC (Students' Non-Violent Coordinating Committee), SCLC (Southern Christian Leadership Conference), and CORE (Congress for Racial Equality) broke with the NAACP tradition of legal maneuvering and use of established channels and set out to organize masses of black people for political action.

The civil rights movement *did* achieve a degree of success. What is important in our consideration here is that it succeeded in changing the consciousness of large numbers of black people in this country. We are not likely again to meet the "Yeh sir, Massah" response and mentality among our black brothers and sisters. The "supplicating, whining tone" and enforced phrases of submission described by Myrdal in 1944 have been changed to a strong and defiant "I am black and I am proud" stance. Although black Americans are still far from having achieved status, income, power on a par with the white middle-class majority here, at least now they are claiming it for themselves. These are the preconditions for any struggle of liberation—awareness, self-respect, and determination. Without them one can go nowhere. With them, one can at the very least get on one's way.

We shall discuss, at a later point, why it is that blacks are no more than on their way and, indeed, seem to have met with obstacles and frustrations that they are helpless to overcome. The example of the civil rights movement is instructive in many respects, yet the parallel should not be overdrawn. We may learn from its failures— or its limitations—as well as from its accomplishments. For now, it is the change in consciousness among blacks brought about by civil rights activists that we are interested in.

We should not forget that, at the point when the civil rights movement got under way, black activists and leaders were as strictly excluded from decision-making positions in American society as women are at present. They had no newspapers, no radio stations, no TV networks, and no approved political springboards from which to launch their drive and communicate their message. The groups were as small and neglected as they were brave and dedicated. Their first problem was to get people to *listen*—to establish communication with their own people and to open up a dialogue with white America. The word had to get out; the vital and shocking call for resistance, for unity, for new actions had to be *heard* by their black brothers and sisters.

Not only did the black activists of the fifties and sixties have to fight the massive indifference and ingrained prejudices of white citizens, they had also to deal with apathy, subservience, and fear among their own people. The objective fact of oppression was obvious enough, it is true, yet there were still a good number of blacks who shied away from any confrontation with it. It was not just the white racist who denounced "the outside agitators." Among the rank and file of blacks, it took years to break down the defensive posture and the ingrained reluctance to fully admit to and deal with one's own oppression. Again, the problem of feminists today offers a striking parallel.

The way to tackle that first hurdle was—and is—*agitation:* expose the nature and extent of oppression; deal with it forthrightly and forcefully, pointing to the clash between expressed ideals and present reality; react to it with the anger and the resolve to change it that is entirely appropriate within the context of American democratic values; hold forth to the individuals suffering from oppression the injustice inherent in their situation; paint the picture in strokes as vivid and bold as realistically possible; call on their sense of righteousness and their buried resentments and make it possible for them to express the anger so long suppressed. Then—go on to organize and to act in the political arena.

Such a recipe has been followed by a variety of activists through time. But for blacks, as for women, the problem was: How does one agitate for social change *in a mass society* where the communication media are foreclosed to one's own use? There were—as there usually are—not nearly enough committed activists to go around for a national organizing drive launched with practically no money and little access to the media. There were—as there are—tens of millions to be reached and innumerable, confusing events and problems competing for their attention. And there were—as there are—no more than a few thousand activists willing and able to do the time-consuming ground work, the door-to-door organizing that is the main alternative to access to the media.

A shortcut had to be found. It was the same for the civil rights movement as for the antiwar movement a few years later: Political demonstrations, boycotts, sit-ins, civil disobedience—every tactic still available to "out-groups" in the political system had to be used. The catchword was *news.* To get the attention of the media, it was not enough to be right, to be moral, to be responsible; one had to be, above all, *news-worthy.* And one becomes news-worthy if the issue is raised dramatically, if the challenge is posed vividly, if one's cause is demonstrated boldly. That is something no mass media in a free society can resist. Where requests to cover meetings and speeches or to broadcast messages for reformist and radical activists will fall on the very dead ears of status-quo-oriented editors and news chiefs, the confrontations initiated by activists contain too much drama, too much portent for change to be ignored.

Getting coverage for demonstrations and unconventional political tactics may be a two-edged sword: Without it a social protest movement in a mass society will never grow beyond infancy. With it, there might be a serious backlash to contend with. But if the movement has a moral base, if it speaks to real, compelling social needs and widely accepted principles, it cannot help but attain new followers and sympathizers by its exposure in the media.

It is crucial to understand, as E. E. Schattschneider has pointed out, that in a democracy it is *the loser* in a conflict situation who has an interest in exposing the issue.[6] Where power and privilege are grossly and unevenly divided, the "outs" have no alternative other than to enlist in their cause a sufficiently large number of people to upset the balance. In our society, this *can* be done through nonrevolutionary, though not always nonviolent, means. But the conflict, if it is to engage more citizens on the side of the "outs," must first become *visible*. It is those who benefit from the institutional arrangements in effect who have an interest in keeping the conflict out of the public arena. Where there is universal suffrage and electoral competition, the involvement of greater numbers of citizens in a conflict carries with it real risks to power elites. From their point of view, the *scope* of the conflict must be contained.

We must recognize, as well, that there are many devices available to power elites to minimize and discredit issues not to their liking. In the case of women's rights, the means used most often is *ridicule*. In the media and in the male-dominated society generally, women's protests are first belittled and made to appear silly, incongruous, and unnecessary. To repeat just a few of the choice phrases fondly repeated among the antifeminists, women activists are depicted as "bra-less bubbleheads" or hysterical man-haters suffering from "menopausal rage." The choicest of all—"Lesbian Communist In-

6. E. E. Schattschneider, *The Semi-Sovereign People* (New York: Holt, Rinehart and Winston, 1969).

tellectuals"—succeeds in bringing together in holy, triumphant union the most rabid and irrational prejudices of the day. Usually, the familiar negative images of women are drawn on in these put-downs. Woman's emotionalism, irrationality, bitchiness, frivolity—all the typical sexist images form a useful basis for attack.

Against the barrage of weapons available to the antifeminists, women activists have only their cause and their commitment to it. But it is a cause that rests firmly on the body of principles long accepted as democratic and wholly American. And feminists have, it must not be forgotten, the potentially greater numbers—53.3 percent of the citizens—a force quite sufficient to transform political and social institutions and the very life style of this nation, with or without male allies.

But of course there will be male allies, just as surely as there will be female opponents, for quite a while yet. One can always find "cracks in the monolith," to begin with—sympathizers, joiners, advocates for the cause with access and influence in the mass media and educational institutions. Above all, there will be supporters of the cause of women—whether for opportunistic or idealistic reasons—among decision-makers in government. The issue is too clear and the cause too much in line with widely expressed ideals for it to be *long* resisted by political and social progressives of this nation. And too, we must remember that women constitute the only minority that lives with the master race, in Helen Hacker's perceptive comment. Male opponents of women's rights may have to confront wives, sisters, daughters, even mothers. A concerned father is particularly vulnerable, if it can be demonstrated, *as it can be,* that his daughter's chance for a more fulfilling and secure life is significantly reduced by the perpetuation of sexist practices.

Converts will come as women demonstrate their seriousness and get their messages through to the public. It is important that leaders in the movement keep in mind the need not to step too far ahead of the main body of citizens. Antifamily, hate-male campaigns are strictly nonproductive both on the political and, in the long run, on the personal level. Although bold maneuvers, inventive campaigns, and dramatic challenges will have to be used to get the attention of the media, the tactics must be directed at *more* than that. They must be aimed at drawing to the movement *new* recruits and making possible the coalition with other "out-groups."

Women have causes in common both with other minorities and with blue-collar, technical, and sales workers in general, as shown in earlier chapters. What is interesting here is that neither the minorities nor the groups of workers we are talking about can by themselves obtain a majority coalition. But if they are joined with a substantial group of women, newly conscious of their rights and needs, the possibility for such a coalition is by no means remote. What has plagued the civil rights movement in recent years is the seeming impossibility of going beyond the advances made for blacks with a promising cultural and educational background. The bulk of black people are very little better off, socially and economically, than they were a decade ago, but the movement is unable to get off its present dead center until it can join in mass action to bring about thorough system-wide change. The situation is or will be the same for other minorities. Confrontation can bring about the modifications and improvements necessary to co-opt the activists and pacify rebelling groups, but for the government to transform itself to bring the present "out-groups" fully into the system, socially and economically, politicians will have to be shown the gradual but certain build-up of a voting majority.

As protests and confrontation politics continue—and there are few signs of any let-up—a new political awakening is emerging among the activists. It becomes increasingly clear that none of the rebelling groups can gain their aims without allies. Any broad strategy for change requires cooperation with carefully selected groups in and out of power. Well-defined group interests are essential to the process; the forceful and effective presentation of these in the public arena and by use of the mass media cannot help but draw new followers. As social ferments continue, other "out-groups" will go through a political awakening and before long the so-called "silent" majority, meaning the status-quo-oriented and presumably content bloc of voters hitherto dominating the political scene, will be reduced to a minority. It is not this group, but the *silenced ones,* that we have to worry about. The resurrection of democratic politics and the creation of social democracy in the United States require that they now prepare for an invasion into the system.

Whether feminists and their allies in the end choose to make use of the present party structure or to create a new one will depend on developments in the near future. Chances are that as the movement grows in numbers and proves itself capable of effective political organizing, politicians within both major parties will soon be on the scene trying to woo the members to their side by promises of support for their program. The danger of co-optation is ever present and, for women, it carries with it a very special risk. The tendency of men to take over and dominate any group made up mainly of women and the inclination so long inbred in women to accept this practice have to be confronted and stopped in every instance. Women have to come into their own, have to discover their abilities and learn to take direction of their own fates without the supervision and guidance of men. "Cooperation, yes—co-optation, no" must be a rallying cry throughout the movement, if women are to transform their self-concepts and gain the self-respect they are so desperately in need of.

"Scratch a woman, and you will find a feminist!" comments Aileen Hernandez, 1970 president of NOW, meaning that any woman made to reflect on her own oppression will end up *as* angry and *as* set on change as are the activists of the movement. That is, indeed, the greatest hope for all who want to see the liberated society come about. If the "impotent rage" of American women can be changed to controlled anger and firm resolve, there will be no stopping of the feminist rebellion. Among those who find that a somewhat frightening prospect, let it be remembered that *a democracy ought not to fear its majority.*

APPENDIX 1

America, Gunnar Myrdal points out, has a more explicit political creed than any other Western nation. In the first chapter of *An American Dilemma*,[1] his now classic study of the Negro problem of this country, Myrdal shows how all vehicles of communication are mobilized to indoctrinate every American with the principles in this American system of ideals. The "American Creed" is taught in the schools, preached from the pulpits, announced by judges in their decisions. Editorials, articles, and public addresses all reflect the same idealism, and even oppressed minorities, like black Americans, share in the creed, pleading with it for their rights and even half-believing that it actually guides America. There is also some evidence, as will be shown in chapter 7 of this book, that women hold to this Creed more firmly and have greater faith in its guiding role than do men.

The ideals expressed in this Creed are quite simply those of the dignity of the individual, fundamental equality, and certain inalienable rights to freedom, justice, and fair opportunity. These are the very principles written into the Declaration of Independence, the Preamble to the Constitution, the Bill of Rights, and the constitutions of the states. Myrdal's achievement in writing *American Dilemma* lies not least in his demonstrating how these ideals are active realities, forming by themselves a dominant social trend. While Americans do not live up to the Creed in practice, sins against it are, on the other hand, loudly and incessantly proclaimed

1. Gunnar Myrdal, *American Dilemma: The Negro Problem and Modern Democracy* (New York: Harper & Brothers, 1942), p. 22.

and lamented. It is the moral tension between ideals and practice regarding the treatment of black citizens particularly that Myrdal refers to as *the* American dilemma. The American Creed is expressive and definite in all respects of importance for the Negro problem, according to his findings, and from the point of view of anyone sharing in that Creed, "the status accorded the Negro in America represents nothing more and nothing less than a century-long lag in public morals."

The status of women in the contemporary United States must equally be seen as presenting a moral as well as a political dilemma to Americans. In this case, as well as in the case of black citizens, we are dealing with a national problem that cuts sharply through the whole body politic. And for us, just as for Myrdal, "no other set of valuations could serve as adequately as the norm for an incisive formulation of our value premises as can the American Creed." [2] It is so widely accepted, has such authority, and is so important as a real social trend that it is acceptable to use it as an "instrumental norm" for research. For, as Myrdal so convincingly demonstrates, the final solution to the value problem in social sciences generally must be to introduce human valuations openly and rationally into theoretical and practical research to give such research direction and purpose. At the same time, the value premises must be tested as to the relevance and significance in the society studied.

This latter task has already been admirably performed by Myrdal, and the historical records of the civil rights movement in the last decade gives ample evidence for his earlier finding, that the American Creed is itself part of the social reality, being constantly called on by oppressed minorities fighting for their rights within this system. It should be added, however, that the ideals referred to here are not just American, but Western. They have found their most express articulation in this country, but they are, in essence, nothing but the humane ideals that have matured over the centuries in Western civilization generally.

2. Gunnar Myrdal, *Value in Social Theory: A Selection of Essays on Methodology* (New York: Harper & Brothers, 1958), p. 68.

APPENDIX 2

The concept of class varies as widely as do theories of class and, as two authorities on the subject have conceded,[1] the discussions concerning the term are often academic substitutes for a real conflict over political orientations. The term "class" was initially used to simply distinguish social strata by their rank or wealth, but in the nineteenth century it emerged as an analytical category which has meaning only in the context of a theory of class. According to Karl Marx's model of class analysis, it is not permissible to interchangeably use the terms class, stratum, rank, and position. Outside of class, these terms refer merely to groupings of people who occupy similar positions on a hierarchical scale in respect to such characteristics as income, prestige, and style of life; they are therefore nothing but descriptive categories. Marx's concept of class, on the other hand, contains a view of interest groups emerging from certain structural conditions that are subject to modification and change through the conflict between these same groups. Marx differs from former stratification analysts—and from present-day functionalists—in his insistence that the nature of the distributive system, and thereby the existence of classes, is determined by the productive system. As the productive system changes, the distributive system responds, but it is the classes that are the basic units in this process of evolution.

1. S. M. Lipset and Reinhard Bendix, "Social Status and Social Structure," *British Journal of Sociology* 11 (1951).

To Marx it is class conflict which brings about the institutional changes required for progress to take place. For a comprehensive and insightful discussion of theories of class, with a particular emphasis on Marx, see Ralf Dahrendorf, *Class and Class Conflict in Industrial Society* (Stanford: Stanford University Press, 1959).

In this study, the distinction between stratum and class is accepted, though at this point in the text it is left as an open question whether women on their own constitute merely a different stratum, or whether there are, in fact, such distinct structural factors in operation as to warrant use of the concept class in regard to working women. In that case, the concept of under class may indeed be the most appropriate one, signifying that members of this grouping are not just inferior in terms of their share of income, status and power, but are generally viewed as subjects by members of the male master class.

It has been suggested that the special and highly disadvantaged position of women in the stratification system makes applicable the designation of *caste;* a closed social grouping into which a person is born and required to stay for life. The rank or social position of a caste member cannot be changed through personal qualities or achievement.[2] Undeniably, there are facts which tend to show the existence of a caste system in regard to women, yet, at this point in time it appears too extreme an explanation. There are too many exceptions to the rule, too many "loophole women" [3] for us to take seriously the suggestion that we are here confronted with the most rigid of stratification systems in existence.

2. For a thorough discussion of caste systems and other forms of stratification, see Gerhard Lenski, *Power and Privilege: A Theory of Social Stratification* (New York: McGraw-Hill Book Co., 1966).
3. Caroline Bird, *Born Female* (New York: Pocket Books, 1969).

INDEX

DATE DUE

OCT 3 1972			
FEB 9 1973			
MAR 1 2 1973			
APR 1 6 1973			
DEC 5 1973			
DEC 1 7 1973			
FEB 1 0 1977			
APR 2 9 1977			
APR 5 1978			
MAR 2 4 1981			
JUL 2 0 1984			
MAR 5 - 1992			
DE 8 '95			
GAYLORD			PRINTED IN U.S.A.